What people are saying about …

RESCUE

"I had anticipated that Justin's book *Rescue* was going to be an insightful look at the world of brotherhood relationships. What I did not anticipate was being drawn in to an adventure that would inspire and deeply challenge me. In today's world there has never been a greater need and opportunity to awaken men to the call for genuine brotherhood relationships. I encourage you as a man to go through this book with another man or as a leader of men to have all your guys go through it together. I can guarantee that your lives will never be the same."

Randy (RT) Phillips, former president of
Promise Keepers, cofounder of CORE, men's
pastor at LifeFamily Church, Austin, Texas

"We men struggle today with distractions, isolation, greed, addiction, and sin—and they keep us from becoming the leaders we need to be in our homes, workplaces, and churches. Fortunately, Jesus is always here to help us. And his rescue comes so often through people with his Spirit in their hearts, through community, through a group of men. We need men who will journey alongside us, helping us live in freedom, not fear. Justin Camp's book *Rescue* will help you cultivate precisely this kind of brotherhood. It'll equip you to identify *your* brothers and forge relationships that last a lifetime. Most importantly, his book will deepen your relationship with Jesus and teach you to allow his rescuing presence into your life. I highly recommend it."

Tim Lukei, men's pastor at
Mariners Church, Irvine, California

"If you're looking to live a life on purpose and in God's victory, Justin Camp will show you how. In his new book, *Rescue*, he moves beyond traditional definitions and provides a field guide for living in *authentic* masculine community—for living in *true* friendship with *real* brothers-in-arms. *Rescue* will be our church's go-to book for building men's community."

Dr. Kevin Trick, men's pastor at
Centre Street Church, chaplain with the
Calgary Police Service, Alberta, Canada

"Having spent one year of my life as an Air Force pilot of the Super Jolly Green Giant (HH-53) rescue helicopter in Vietnam, I know how intense and exciting a rescue experience can be. Through his incredible rescue stories, Justin Camp has set the stage for the greatest rescue of all—God's loving rescue of the human heart and soul. Biblical foundation, quotations by God's saints through the ages, practical guidance on building community are all captured in his new book, *Rescue*. Justin has given us a spiritual jewel, a Holy Spirit–led tool that will help us build personal rescue teams to save us through Jesus Christ the Lord."

Chaplain (Maj. Gen.) Charles C. Baldwin,
US Air Force, Chief of Chaplains (ret.)

"Ever since our dismissal from Eden, God has been calling men from a life of lying, hiding, and faking to a peloton of grace. Justin, in his unassailable storytelling, biblically and practically unveils to us our need for unpretentious community. Quoting Bonhoeffer, he tells us, 'When I go to my brother, I am going to God.' Sure to be a powerful contribution to God's work in the lives of men!"

Chaplain (Maj. Gen.) Steven A. Schaick, DMin,
US Air Force, Chief of Chaplains (ret.)

"An enduring strategy of the enemy of our soul is to push us into isolation from God and spiritual communities, and have us believe that we can throttle through alone all that life throws at us. Justin Camp's book *Rescue* is a clarion call for men to step out of that lie by boldly moving into close relationships with a band of believing brothers. Through gripping stories, Justin teaches how to contend for this kind of brotherhood and experience the authentic life

Jesus invites us to with confidence, courage, and hope. I highly recommend *Rescue*."

Chaplain (Capt.) Gary P. Weeden, US Navy, Command Chaplain of US European Command, Chaplain of the US Coast Guard (ret.)

"Justin Camp's *Rescue* brings into sharp focus humanity's need for dramatic and cosmic rescue. But how does one obtain it? Where does one go? What if previous attempts to reform have failed? Is there any hope? The answer—*always good news!*—is that God in the crucified and risen Christ Jesus is the giver of all mercy and the redeemer of all broken lives. He's the one who answers our prayers for rescue every time, and Justin's book helps us find that rescue through the supportive kinship of other people."

Chaplain (Col.) Tom Decker, US Army (ret.), former smokejumper for the US Forest Service, author of *Fire Starters*

"'So others may live.' That's the US Coast Guard rescue swimmer motto. When folks are in distress, when it's dark, stormy, and people are praying to God for help, rescue swimmers go out into that danger. We answer the call. We get to be guardian angels, dropping in from orange helicopters hovering overhead. It's not so different in Christian community. As Jesus said, 'Greater love has no one than this, that someone lay down his life for his friends.' Therefore, the motto of every men's group should be 'So *brothers* may live.' In this hard and unforgiving world, we followers of Jesus get to be guardian angels for one another in our everyday lives. Because God's very Spirit lives within our hearts, we get to sacrifice ourselves and participate in Jesus' rescuing work—pulling our friends out of isolation, addiction, and sin and helping them find community, freedom, and joy. Justin Camp's new book, *Rescue*, teaches men how to build and maintain just this kind of brotherhood. I pray that men read this book and begin loving one another as Jesus loves us."

Chief Petty Officer Ken Kiest, Aviation Survival Technician, US Coast Guard (ret.)

"What hell week is for Navy SEAL training, this captivating book is for authentic Christian community. Mentally tough yet deeply inspiring. Every page of *Rescue* holds you spellbound for true Christian community. Like a Navy SEAL trainee bonds with his swim buddy, every Christian man must have a forever rescue team. Although Justin Camp's book is written for men, women too will embrace its no-fluff, hard-hitting invitation for Christ-inspired relationships."

L. C. Fowler, Basic Underwater Demolition SEAL Class 89, author of *Dare to Live Greatly*

"*Rescue* is a bold invitation to masculine initiation and the path to recovering a quality of life beyond telling. Having put in the long and hard miles himself, Justin offers generously from his own story with courage, love, and vulnerability. Those who choose to receive the invitation in *Rescue* will become the wholehearted men to whom God can entrust the care of his kingdom."

Morgan Snyder, author of *Becoming a King*, vice president of Wild at Heart, founder of BecomeGoodSoil.com

"I'm thirty-one and I've officially been to more funerals than years I've been alive. Over twenty of the funerals were suicides and drug overdoses. Perhaps your own experience isn't so extreme, yet we all see the increased presence of depression and anxiety, along with loneliness and shame, in our own lives and the lives of those we cherish. The natural question is *where is God?* And *what is he doing?* Justin looks at these very questions and takes us on a pilgrimage of rescue, a pilgrimage I find myself needing every day."

Shane James O'Neill, editorial director of Proven Ministries

RESCUE

✚

JUSTIN CAMP

RESCUE

WHEN GOD'S CAVALRY ARRIVES TO DELIVER YOU FROM QUIET DESPERATION

DAVID **C** COOK

transforming lives together

RESCUE
Published by David C Cook
4050 Lee Vance Drive
Colorado Springs, CO 80918 U.S.A.

Integrity Music Limited, a Division of David C Cook
Brighton, East Sussex BN1 2RE, England

The graphic circle C logo is a registered trademark of David C Cook.

Library of Congress Control Number 2021940966
ISBN 978-0-8307-7872-0
eISBN 978-0-8307-8224-6

© 2021 Justin Camp

The Team: Wendi Lord, Michael Covington, Jeff Gerke,
James Hershberger, Jack Campbell, Susan Murdock
Cover Design: Nick Lee
Cover Image: Getty Images

Printed in the United States of America
First Edition 2021

1 2 3 4 5 6 7 8 9 10

081821

To Jenn and Abby and all
those who love so well.

To the men of the Oaks, the Deep, the
Table, and the Cave too. My brothers.

I will never leave you nor forsake you.
— promise from God

No one has seen God, ever. But if we love one another,
God dwells deeply within us, and his
love becomes complete in us.
— truth from John

CONTENTS

A PRAYER OF SHELTER AND SHADOW

Ar scáth a chéile a mhaireas na daoine.
~ It is in the shelter of each other that the people live.
~ It is in the shadow of each other that the people live.
We know that sometimes we are alone,
and sometimes we are in community.
Sometimes we are in shadow,
and sometimes we are surrounded by shelter.
Sometimes we feel like exiles—
in our land, in our languages and in our bodies.
And sometimes we feel surrounded by welcome.
As we seek to be human together,
may we share the things that do not fade:
generosity, truth-telling, silence, respect and love.
And may the power we share
be for the good of all.
We honour God, the source of this rich life.
And we honour each other, story-full and lovely.
Whether in our shadow or in our shelter,
may we live well
and fully
with each other.
Amen.

// Pádraig Ó Tuama, poet

BEFORE YOU START

I want to tell you a story, and it begins with eight words: "There are no atheists in the fox holes."[1] The first person likely to have uttered that enduring phrase is one 1st Lt. William Cummings. He reportedly spoke it in a field sermon delivered to troops huddled in 1942 on the Philippine peninsula of Bataan, the site of the heroic and horrific American and Filipino last stand against Japanese invasion.

Lieutenant Cummings was an Army chaplain from San Francisco who went down as a legend of the Pacific Theater of World War II. Soldiers said he "radiated an unalterable goodness and gentleness."[2] But Cummings wasn't naive toward the awfulness of war. He saw things. He experienced things. He knew fear. *Real fear.* Bone-shaking fear. For he too stood on that rocky promontory. He too stood among those brave but ill-fated men. Sick and starving. Outnumbered and surrounded. Fighting, yes, but really just waiting for inevitable death or capture by an overwhelming and unforgiving adversary.

Cummings also knew suffering. *Real suffering.* Hope-splintering suffering. After the Japanese Imperial Army captured him and 75,000 soldiers at Bataan, he was cast into the Japanese war prison system. He endured horrid conditions in hellish camps for nearly three years before being loaded onto a series of ships bound for Japan. Against all odds, he survived two aerial bombardments from American pilots unaware of those ships' precious POW cargo. Two prison vessels sank; twice he was rescued. His Japanese captors then put the surviving prisoners onto a third. Conditions were so appalling, though, that before the vessel could reach Japan, Cummings succumbed to "starvation and exposure."[3]

An American serviceman described a moment belowdecks with Cummings in the days before the chaplain's death, down in those freezing and filthy compartments:

> Suddenly from the depths of the hold I heard a voice like the voice of God. Father Cummings began to speak. The sound was clear and resonant and made me feel he was talking to me alone. The men became quiet.
>
> "Our Father Who art in heaven, hallowed be Thy name. Thy kingdom come. Thy will be done on earth as it is in heaven...." The voice went on. Strength came to me as I listened to the prayer, and a certain calmness of spirit.
>
> "Have faith," he continued. "Believe in yourselves and in the goodness of one another. Know that in yourselves and in those that stand near you, you see the image of God. For mankind is in the image of God."[4]

Cummings was a man of prayer. Both on Bataan and in captivity, he undoubtedly cried out to God in desperation and petition. But he also influenced those around him with uncommon peace and confidence. Even as friendly bombs mercilessly fell, his trust in God never wavered. Even as death came for him in dankness and darkness, he held his ground. He stayed on mission. Wrote another soldier, "He died as he would have wanted to die, praying to the God he believed in, to the God that gave him strength."[5]

So what's the deal? Why was he different? How did Cummings come by this calm and assurance? How did he *know* that God was listening, looking after, caring for him even in his deep suffering?

Cummings was different because he knew a secret.

Wracked with fear or agony, finding ourselves hard-pressed on every side, nearly all of us will call out for rescue, believers or not. Whether facing physical danger, financial distress, relationship heartache, public humiliation, burnout at work, termination of employment, depression, addiction, incarceration, or any other kind of severe trial, most of us will look to the heavens and cry out in silent prayer. We'll make our desperate pleas to God.

Cummings saw it firsthand on Southeast Asian battlefields. No atheists in fox holes.

And yet. Even in the worst tribulation, even experiencing awful trauma, though we call out to him, God can still feel ethereal. Elusive. *Less-than-real?*

If only we could, in those situations, reach out our hands and actually grip Jesus' hand of rescue. If only we could hear his reassuring voice, sound waves vibrating in our ears, telling us, *Everything's going to be okay*. If only turning to him meant actually turning our mortal bodies and finding him there—right there physically, right there with us in our grim circumstances.

Then things would be different.

But he never *is* there physically, is he? And that's the problem. We never know for sure that God is actually listening when we pray. Whether he's even heard us. Whether he's truly coming to save us. Whether he's arrived already.

Have you ever wondered such things?

Let's get back to the secret that Lieutenant Cummings held in his heart. The one that invigorated his spirit. Lifted his weary soul. The one that made him, in so many ways, impervious to his surroundings.

What was it? What *was* this secret? Well, that's precisely what the coming chapters are all about. I will, however, give you a sneak peek. What Cummings knew, and what most of us do not, is how to actually find our ethereal God. He knew the formula for truly laying hold of the God of the Universe, for grasping him actually and tangibly, and for receiving all of his help in our darkest hours. (And in all our *other* hours too, actually.) Cummings knew that this precious secret has something to do with men gathering under the name of Jesus Christ.

He knew it.

And, brother, in these pages, you'll discover the secret too.

Rescue is structured around a handful of stories. Each chapter has one. These include five fascinating accounts of five very different kinds of rescue teams—Swiss alpine search-and-rescue squads, US Coast Guard helicopter rescue units, the men and women at the International Submarine Escape and Rescue Liaison Office, US interagency hotshot crews, and the dauntless chaplaincy corps serving inside the walls of our state and federal prisons. These are intriguing tales of amazing men and women. Intrepid people who regularly move *toward* danger, not away. Men and women who lay everything on the line every day for their fellow human. People who voluntarily place themselves into situations fraught with danger and say to the rest of us, "You don't need to be afraid, not on my watch."

The first rescue team profiled will come in chapter 2, after my own story kicks things off. And each of these profiles opens with a short piece of fiction. In those sections, all names, characters, events, and incidents are purely the products of my imagination. Any resemblance to actual persons, living or dead, or actual events is entirely coinciden-tal. I wrote them to provide hopefully honest and honoring pictures of these revered teams.

Embedded in these great stories—and in the chapters that follow each profile—you *will* find Lieutenant Cummings's secret. So go ahead. Search for it. Hunt for it in the chapters as each builds on the prior one. (It won't be hard to find.) Also, at the close of each of these chapters, you'll find a section entitled "Clip In." The simple exercises found there will turn the focus to you. Take your time with them.

These exercises will teach you to take Cummings's priceless secret into your own heart and live it out.

Trust me, brother: we all need this. If you're facing anguish right now or just a bit of angst, you need it. If you're caught in addiction or chronic sin or just want to make a few changes in your life, you need it. If you're in a season of anxiety and depression or simply a time of aimlessness, you need it. If you're feeling alone and lonely or just a bit disconnected, you need what this book has to offer.

God's got something extraordinary for you in this book. He is, right now, inviting you into a whole new kind of life. A life full of wisdom and joy, connection and confidence. A hearty life but a peaceful one too. A life fulfilled, devoted to loving God, loving the people around you, and receiving all of their love right back.

This kind of life is *absolutely* available to you. Let me show you.

Justin Camp
San Francisco Peninsula

LOVE'S ALL WE NEED

I wanna live safe
I wanna live sound
I wanna be free
But I wanna be found

// Kelly Bibeau, songwriter

FAUX STONE AND LEATHER
AND FREEDOM

A man holds stitched gray leather in a death grip. Not that he notices. His neck and attention are straining; his eyes fixed on one thing: the stoplight regulating the traffic flowing across his field of vision. The *whooshes* of cars passing—rubber on asphalt—are amplified by the rain. His wipers flap intermittently, streaking drizzle mixed with dust mixed with pollen across his windshield. *Come on.* He sits.

The sun is still above the horizon and will be for another thirty minutes, but he can barely tell. The gloom is thick. Headlights and taillights reflect and refract off the wet streets and through the windshield's watery film. *Come on!*

If he were, at this moment, willing to crack even one of the car's windows, he'd be struck by something he loves: the wonderfully rich scent of recently rained-upon coastal live oaks and Northern California bunch grasses. But he keeps the windows rolled up.

One of the man's too-long-ago-polished leather chukka boots presses the brake pedal but lightly, his foot just itching to make the switch—to hit the gas, to gun it—as soon as he catches sight of that red light for the cross traffic. *Yellow. Red. There it is.* He and his black vehicle launch into the intersection. The engine in this thing is big enough to take most comers, but no one's looking to race today.

RPMs soar for two blocks. The man then slams on the brakes and cranks the wheel, just able to catch the left-turn signal for a tight U-turn. He guns the engine again, coming the opposite way on the street down which he'd just sped. About halfway down the block, he jerks the wheel once more and flies up a ramp to his right, into a lot. He considers parking close but opts for a space on the far end, about fifty yards from the building entrance. He comes in fast, angling his car between the white lines, jams the brakes once again, slides it into park, and yanks up the parking brake, all with smooth, efficient motions.

And then he sits in the silence. The rain is too light to make a sound inside the car.

Am I really doing this? Do I really need to be here?

More silence. He looks down at his phone. It's 5:32 p.m.

"All right," he says out loud.

He opens the door and steps out into the misty cold of early March. He slams the door, then hits the lock button on his key fob as he hustles and thumps toward the building. No idea what to expect, he pushes through two sets of glass doors. Once inside, he's hit with the less-than-awesome smell of an office building atrium fountain. Across the dark space, though, warm light and laughter spill from a conference room.

He navigates mini-canals, a bridge, and tiled planter boxes with fake palms and ferns, then he hears those same glass doors open and close behind him. Probably another man headed where he's headed. *No turning back now.* Defenses high, he approaches the door. He pauses for less than a second, then steps in.

Seven men gather around a large conference table engrossed in banter about something they clearly think is quite funny. The meeting hasn't yet begun. "Hey, brother!" One of the men welcomes him. After handshakes and quick intros, he slips into a seat at the table. He hunches down and begins rocking slightly and silently as the guys enjoy an easy camaraderie and seem to be waiting for more men to show.

Five more arrive, including the man who came in right behind him, and then things get rolling. Jason, the leader of the group, opens with a prayer and leads the group into something he calls "Praise and Confession." He encourages each man to offer praise to God (for something good that happened in the past week) and confession (of something not so good that each man did during the past week that he needs to get off his chest). *Jeez. Really?*

The exercise begins on the other side of the room—thankfully. As he listens, feeling like it must be obvious that he's the newest person to the group, it isn't the praise items that surprise him; it's the confessions. These men reveal things that people never do. They talk about things no one talks about. They don't speak long, but they talk about real fears and real failures. They talk about sin—their own. They talk about alcohol and pornography and serious anger. *Whoa!*

His turn approaches, but he's not too worried. He'll get through it all right. He's good at saying all the right things. But then he notices his heart rate begins to speed. Something unexpected wells up. It's like he doesn't want to BS it this time. Shoving that impulse down, he plays it safe. He talks about his kids and makes up an incident where his temper was short. And when he's done, he leans back and stops rocking. He listens to the last few men go. He hears their words but retreats into his mind. Into his heart.

Something is happening.

It's dawning on the man; even though he's been here only a few minutes, he's found something. Something important. Necessary. Something of tremendous value and power. Something he's been searching and grasping for his entire life. He just never knew that *this* is what he's been looking for all those years. But he knows now. And he somehow senses that this thing is probably going to be part of his life now, for the rest of his life.

The man has just stumbled upon Lieutenant Cummings's secret.

That was me.

I'd known Brenden through church. Our wives had gotten to know each other first. He and Amy have three kids too, about the same ages as ours. And it was Brenden who invited me to try out his men's group. It was also his "Hey, brother" I received when I walked into that conference room, his voice revealing his surprise that I'd actually turned up. Because that wasn't the only time he'd invited me. He'd asked me to come lots of times over a period of years.

But life was crazy back then. Jennifer and I were chronically tired and stressed out. When I finally accepted Brenden's invitation, our boys were seven and five; our little girl had just turned three. My venture capital career was in full gear; I was trying my best to build a firm and make sound investments. Jennifer was hard at work as a stay-at-home mom and leading a women's ministry at our church too. We were also leading a couples' Bible study together.

We were a team, but our hearts were out of sync. I worked long hours, anxious about whether I could earn enough money to support this new family. Worried deeply about how we would pay for everything: a Bay Area mortgage, property taxes, health insurance, orthodontists, cars, college. We weren't saving much. When anyone would talk about their "nest egg," I'd feel a twinge of adrenaline in my heart. *Work harder.*

I felt those same twinges around my health too. During that season, I was constantly worried about some new ache, focused on some new pain. Tests would turn up negative, but that never did much to quell my anxiety. Lying in bed at night, I'd come up with elaborate and seemingly credible explanations for what might be going on, though nothing ever was.

Measuring fear on a scale from 0 to 10—0 being, well, 0 and 10 being debilitating—I would guess that, between worries about finances and health and not having what it takes to be the sole provider for my family, I was walking around in those days at a reliable 6.5.

Despite all of that, every time Brenden asked me to try out his group, I had excuses. I just couldn't envision how it could possibly be very helpful. I also couldn't imagine adding one more thing to our already-filled calendar. So I declined. Every time. Except that one. And on that cold day in early March of 2009, when the anxiety and discontent felt particularly intense, almost unbearable, I relented and agreed to *one* meeting.

The group met in a conference room in an office building where Brenden's friend Jason worked. It has since been demolished and replaced, but it sat very close to the geographic epicenter of Silicon Valley. It was classic '80s style, the exterior mostly darkly tinted glass. The interior was full of glass brick walls, seafoam-green tile, chrome accents, and marble surfaces. Walking in felt like a time warp—to a place I thought I'd never want to visit.

Inside that conference room, it was the same. Everything was over the top. The imposing table could seat ten to twelve. The chairs were big and leather and supremely comfortable. I've never seen chairs like those anywhere else. But the best/worst part of the room was that the walls, the ceiling, the whole room, even the wastebaskets, were covered in gray faux-stone wallpaper. And that's how the group got its name: *the Cave.*

After only my first few moments with the men in that room, I resolved to keep coming. That decision surprised me, given my reluctance going in. And it scared me. I knew that coming back would mean I, too, would have to be as honest about my life as those men were about theirs. But I almost didn't care. Almost. Because I knew I'd found brothers. And though I didn't understand it at the time, I'd found Jesus too—in a way I'd never found him before.

"In him was life, and the life was the light of men" (John 1:4).

For the next twelve months, through these men, Jesus showed me a different way to live. It was life *in* community. With men who would become real friends. Friends who knew the whole story, the good parts of me and the bad. Friends who would pray with and for me—*really pray.* Friends who read Scripture, took it seriously, and tried to apply it to their lives. Friends willing to speak truth to one another, who built each other up. Friends eager to call out gifts and talents and to encourage each other to use them. Friends who held each other accountable and even gently confronted each other on passivity and anything less than full transparency. Friends who, I would learn, would do anything for me.

And that's how, for me, the rescues began.

Jesus, through these men, rescued me from loneliness and shame. Up until those first couple of months at the Cave, I'd been leading a double life. No one knew about my struggles with pornography. No one knew of my self-contempt. But when I began doing what I never thought I could do, when I started confessing, these men accepted me. I expected rejection but got more profound friendship and help and love than I knew was even possible.

And Jesus, through these men, rescued me from isolation and alienation. I'd gone to church all my life, but I had never experienced a close-up, ongoing, one-on-one relationship with Jesus. Until those months, I had assumed that prayer was mostly a one-way deal—me doing all the talking. But the men of the Cave introduced me to something they called "listening prayer." We would lean in to sense God's voice in the silence. They taught me how to hear and discern his *still, small voice* and how to test everything against Scripture.

And Jesus, through these men, rescued me from confusion about my purpose and identity. I was well practiced at bringing my *Who am I? What should I be doing with my life?* questions to the institutions of our culture. I'd become a lawyer and a venture capitalist because, in hundreds of ways, our culture had told me that I should. But the men of the Cave taught me to bring my questions to God instead. They taught me how to begin discovering *real* purpose and *true*, God-given identity.

And then Jesus, through these men, rescued me from my darkest moment.

I had done some writing in college and law school and a bit after graduation. Almost a decade before I joined the Cave, though, I'd decided that writing, while fulfilling in a way that no other endeavor ever was, was simply irresponsible—a distraction from what was most important. I concluded that the only responsible path was to focus on family and career and nothing else.

That was an intense season. All three of our children were born during those years, and I tried to be home and present for Jennifer and our brand-new gang. But everything else, every other minute of my time and ounce of my energy, was devoted to my work. My ambition. And toward the end of that decade was when I first walked into the Cave. Burning out. Needing something to give.

I remember one particular Tuesday evening in January 2010, several months after I'd joined the group. We'd just returned from a family ski vacation in the mountains around Lake Tahoe. I showed up at the Cave exhausted. Having skipped the group for a few weeks around Christmas and New Year's, I was feeling disconnected—from my brothers, from Jesus.

After the opening preliminaries, Jason invited us again into a time of listening prayer. I wasn't really feeling it, though. He encouraged us to ask God about his desires for each of us for the coming year. He opened the prayer, and we closed our eyes and sat for a few minutes in silence.

I remember it feeling a lot like our kids probably feel when Jennifer and I call one of them into our bedroom for a serious talk. When I closed my eyes, my heart was in a posture like, *What, God? What have I done* now? And I sat there for ten seconds, twenty seconds. Then, once I stopped trying to sense anything, a thought came. It was a picture. In my imagination, I saw myself writing again. I was sitting at a laptop in a cabin in the woods by a creek. And I was happy.

My heart softened. *Oh gosh.* I hadn't thought about the vocation of writing for a very long time. I doubt anyone in the room, if they'd opened their eyes, could have seen it, but I was overcome with emotion. To write is one of the deep desires of my heart, but I'd pushed it so far down, I'd pretty much forgotten about it.

If only that could come true! But then reality crept in. I told God that it wasn't possible. My job. My family. *I don't have time.*

Let me *make time, my son. I can do that, you know.* It wasn't an audible voice. It was really just an idea that floated through my mind.

And I knew that I knew. It was a moment of conversation. It was a good Father talking to his weary son, through Jesus and by his Spirit. I'd come into God's presence like a petulant child, and he'd come into mine with overwhelming love.

I answered in the silence. *Please, Father.* It felt like such a tremendous blessing, like just what my worn-out heart needed. And there seemed to be only one appropriate response: an offering back. *Father, I said, I don't want to write about venture capital or business or anything else anymore. I want to write about you.*

And I did. Within a year of joining the Cave, I was writing again. To men. About God.

It started small. I'd sneak out of the office on Fridays during the lunch hour. I'd take my laptop to a nearby coffee shop. It felt good to be putting words together again. Soon, it grew to two hours, then three. God was fulfilling his promise. I hadn't had extra moments in years, but large chunks of time were opening up to me.

In this same season, I was also becoming increasingly dissatisfied with my job in high-tech investing. I enjoyed all the smart people I got to meet. I loved learning about new technologies. I loved supporting other people, helping them realize their dreams. But there was also a sadness I felt in the mornings, driving to the office. I can see now that I was getting tired of trying to be something I wasn't. My priorities were changing too. I was caring less and less about earning and achieving the goals I'd set for myself long ago. I was feeling more and more like an outsider, an alien, in that close-knit industry.

It got to the point that I would dread going into the office in the mornings. Mondays were the worst.

I'd worked so hard to build a firm and earn a reputation, and I was just beginning to see that hard work pay off. All I could think about, though, was my exit strategy. But I couldn't leave. I'd made commitments to my investors—to the people and organizations that had entrusted me and my partners with their money to invest on their behalf. At that point, there were still years of work ahead to invest that money wisely and manage the investments we'd made. I was feeling more and more trapped.

So I did the only thing I could do. I put my head down and muscled through. A couple of years went by, my heart saved by the joys of being with my family, the excitement of joining a band of brothers, and the few hours each week I could spend writing.

But then, in mid-2012, I reached a crossroads. We were coming to the end of our latest venture fund, and I finally had some options. By that time, our firm had allocated all of the money from that fund to specific companies. So my partners and our investors began asking me if and when we would raise another one.

Another fund would certainly be the best source of income for my family, but it would also mean another ten-to-twelve-year commitment. And my heart couldn't bear that. But what else could I do? I hadn't practiced law for over a decade.

And that was when Jesus, through my brothers, came to my rescue again—right when I needed it most.

In my confusion, I decided to hijack an entire Tuesday night meeting. I turned it into my own version of something the Quakers call a "clearness committee." I'd read about the practice in Parker Palmer's book *Let Your Life Speak*. It is, wrote the wise and wonderful Palmer, "a powerful way to rally the strength of community around a struggling soul, to draw deeply from the wisdom within all of us."[1]

Here's how it works: A person wrestling with a decision offers a small group of people a summary of the issues at hand, his feelings about those issues, and any relevant background details. Then a discussion ensues. But the people gathered are, wrote Palmer, "prohibited from suggesting 'fixes'" and can only "pose honest, open questions."[2]

So that's what we did. I told my brothers that I needed to make a choice. I told them I had to figure out how to provide for my family for that next season of life. I told them my options, as I saw them: I could raise another venture fund; I maybe could do a high-tech start-up of my own; or I could start a ministry. I was getting creative. I believed the second one was an option because I'd helped lots of companies get started already. But around the third option, my thinking was vague.

Jenn and I had led a few short-term mission trips at that point and had spent time with people running schools for disadvantaged kids in remote places. I didn't know what I didn't know, but I thought maybe I could do something like that. It was, after all, the only option of the three that didn't cause my heart to sink when I envisioned it.

And that's when the rescue came. When I stopped talking, two of my friends looked at each other and, totally breaking the clearness committee rules (thank God), offered some advice. One of them was Brenden. The other was Chris, another longtime, dear friend of mine.

"I'm not telling you which option you should choose," Chris said. "But whatever you do, you need to be writing."

Then Brenden spoke. "Whatever you do, you need to be writing. First and foremost."

My response was immediate. "Guys, I appreciate it. I would *love* to do that. But I know enough about the economics of the publishing business. It'll be impossible to earn a living and support my family writing books."

Chris leaned forward and looked right into my eyes. "I think you need to not worry about that."

And again, I knew that I knew. What these men were telling me was right and good and true. And I resolved then and there to find a way to write full-time. I decided not to raise another fund and began the process of winding down my venture capital work.

It took six years to complete the transition. There were important obligations to address. But I knew what I wanted to do for the rest of my life. Soon after, Jennifer and I incorporated Gather Ministries, our nonprofit. And each subsequent year, I was able to devote more and more of my time to writing. As I slowly ramped down my venture capital work and ramped up my ministry work, joy and purpose replaced burnout and discontentment.

There is no way I would be doing what I am doing today were it not for my brothers. Were it not for Jesus. Were it not for their coming for me with rescue in their hearts.

Were it not for community.

Father Zosima, the saintly old monk in Fyodor Dostoyevsky's masterwork *The Brothers Karamazov*, said, "Salvation will come from the people."[3] What he meant is that, ever since his ascension two thousand years ago, Jesus rescues us mostly *through* his people—through the flesh-and-blood followers in whom his Spirit dwells.

As a result, we can access Jesus' rescuing power whenever we need it, because his Spirit is all around us. Were he still with us on earth in the physical form of a man, we'd have to mob him, like his first-century followers had to do, in order to gain access to him. But now, we find Jesus by merely finding one of his followers. We actually and truly find *God*—and his incredible saving power—by simply locating a brother or sister.

That's why community is so important. That's why, just before his death and resurrection, Jesus gave his disciples (and us) a new commandment: "that you love one another." "Just as I have loved you," he said, "you also are to love one another" (John 13:34).

Without the love and devotion and acceptance of my brothers, I'd still be alone in my shame, isolated and alienated from God, in a job that I'd grown to hate, having little or no sense of my true, God-given identity. Without brothers willing to come for me, I'd still be trapped somewhere out there in the darkness.

Scripture is clear: we're meant to *be* together, to *do life* together, to *care* for one another, to be *united* with God and our brothers and sisters in Jesus Christ.

And when we are united, then we are strong and healthy and free.

Don't think this is not for you. Brother, you are not alone. None of us is ever alone. Not really. Rich, long-term community is available to each of us, and this book will give you everything you need to do to discover it and build it and maintain it.

If you want to be, you *will* be found. And you *will* be rescued. Again and again.

RECKLESS LOVE

There's no shadow You won't light up
Mountain You won't climb up
...
There's no wall You won't kick down
Lie You won't tear down

Coming after me

// Cory Asbury et al., songwriters

ROTORS AND CARABINERS
AND RADIANCE

Two Americans are in the Swiss Alps. Sean Morris and Scott Murphy are toiling along the Haute Route (*haute* is the French word for "high") that stretches 114 miles from Chamonix, France, to Zermatt, Switzerland. Because they're on skis, they're taking a slightly modified course—a line that's more direct than the one hikers take. Their route skips the usual ups and downs into the various alpine valleys and stays mostly in the mountains.

Mountaineers call this particular version the *Glacier* Haute Route. And as the name indicates, it requires lots of glacier travel. About 40 percent of the route actually lies *on* glaciers. And in six days, Sean and Scott have already traversed eight of them—two just this morning.

Twenty-eight and twenty-nine years old, respectively, closer than brothers, these two men are relishing the opportunity to push themselves physically and share in a great adventure. But Sean planned this particular trip quickly and with a singular purpose: to help a friend get away and get his mind off what's been a tough breakup. Scott met Ashley back in college, and they reconnected two years ago in New York City and have been dating ever since. Well, that is, until seven weeks ago.

Last evening, the two men lingered at a table in the large dining room in the Vignettes Hut and talked late into the night. Built in 1924, then expanded in 1946, Vignettes is a legendary refuge perched high on a cliff, seemingly in the back of beyond. It's maintained by the Swiss Alpine Club and accommodates up to 120 adventurers, offering showers, bathrooms, bunk beds, and hot meals.

But Sean and Scott left the safety of Vignettes this morning. And because of their lively conversation and late night, they got a later-than-expected start on this, the last and most grueling day of their trip. Today's segment climbs through three cols. *Col* is another French word. It means "mountain pass." After the cols, today's portion of the route descends all the way down into the town of Zermatt.

Through fresh snow, the men climb up through the Col de l'Evêque (elevation: 11,129 feet). They can ascend these mountains because the bottoms of their touring skis are covered with "skins"—a mix of mohair and synthetic fur. The fur flattens and glides over the snow when the skis move forward but grips when pushed backward. This allows them to gain footholds in the slick snow and drive up and over alpine passes.

With welcome descents in between, the men make their way through the Col du Mont Brulé (elevation: 10,541 feet) and Col de Valpelline (elevation: 11,706 feet) next. When the pitch is too steep for skinning and they are forced to hike, Sean and Scott strap their skis to their packs and fasten crampons (steel spikes) to their boots.

When they come through the Valpelline pass, a sight catches their hearts. The Matterhorn awash in afternoon sun. That legendary 14,692-foot rock that marks the finish line for their epic trek.

And now, it's all downhill. Sean and Scott just need to cross three remaining glaciers—Stockji, Tiefmatten, and Zmutt—then ski down into Zermatt for a well-earned beer. This last section, known as the Valpelline descent, is one of the best and longest descents in the Alps. It's nearly 10 miles long and has a vertical drop of almost 8,000 feet.

As the guys look down at the Stockji Glacier, they consider fastening safety ropes. This particular glacier is renowned for large crevasses, and conditions are deteriorating a bit in the afternoon sun. But the powder is excellent, and there are tracks from skiers who descended earlier in the day. Sean and Scott reassure themselves: those folks made it down without any problems. So the two friends forgo the ropes. They decide to stick to the safety of the existing tracks but also to cut loose a bit and bomb down this section. They want to make the most of their last day.

Glaciers are massive sheets of ice created by centuries of snowfall that has accumulated and never melted. But they are neither solid nor static. They move like super-slowly flowing rivers, always groaning under their unimaginable weight. Glaciers shift and fracture as they grind over rock, down slopes, and around bends. The resulting cracks are called crevasses, and they can be big—and deep.

Crevasses are tremendous hazards to hikers and skiers. What makes them particularly dangerous, though, is that they can be hidden. Windblown snow can adhere to the top edges of a crevasse—and enough of it can accumulate so that it closes entirely over the top of the crevasse, creating what is called a "snow bridge." When that happens, these frightening fissures become invisible, and glacial surfaces can look like smooth, unbroken snowfields that *must* be safe to cross. And they are safe, sometimes.

The strength of any snow bridge varies based on its thickness and the temperature of the ambient air. A bridge that can support a fully loaded helicopter on a cold day or early morning can become weak and unstable in an afternoon thaw. If the snow thaws enough, the bridge will sag and eventually collapse. When this happens, the underlying crevasses are easy to see and avoid. The thing is, though, snow bridges can weaken even before they begin to sag. In this case, they become death traps; they can give way under a single person's weight.

Because of this danger, mountaineers often traverse glaciers in groups and tether themselves to one another with ropes. They typically spread out and maintain fifty to sixty feet of distance between each other. That way, if one person falls through the snow into a crevasse below, the others can flop onto the surface of the glacier and arrest the victim's fall.

Since Scott and Sean didn't rope up, though, Scott can do nothing to help when the ground opens underneath Sean's skis and he disappears almost without a sound.

Sean plunges into the narrow crack; he struggles and grabs at the crevasse walls. But he finds no purchase. He does find incredible pain, though, as the gap between walls narrows, forcing his left arm over his head, yanking his humerus right out of its socket. Finally, he lands in a clatter and with a dreadful thud—seventy feet down in the deep and dark and cold.

Stunned and bleeding from his forehead, Sean fights to regain his senses. He's on his side amid some of the ice chunks he pulled down as he fell. One of his skis is wedged awkwardly underneath him. The other is nowhere to be seen. Breathing heavily in the thin air, he raises his head and looks around in the darkness.

He can see that he's on some sort of small ledge. Next to him is another drop so deep that all he can see is pitch black. High above him, though, sunlight pours through the opening he just made in the snow. As he tries to gather his thoughts, a strange one comes. *It's beautiful up there.* He becomes momentarily mesmerized by the range of blues captured in the newly illuminated ice. Snapping out of it, he realizes that he cannot move. He's wedged between the two walls. He rests his head on the ice for a moment, trying to regain some strength. Instead, he passes out.

Back up on the surface, Scott doesn't waste a minute. He bites the fingertips of his glove and struggles to free his hand. He unzips his chest pocket and fishes out his cell phone. Coverage has been spotty, so he prays for enough signal. Both men had put the various French and Swiss rescue outfits on speed dial before they'd even left the States. He mashes his wet finger into the dial icon on the touchscreen.

A woman picks up before the first ring even finishes. "Air Zermatt! *Hallo.*"

"Hello! My friend has fallen into a crevasse. We need rescue!"

Switching to English, "A crevasse?"

"Yes. We need rescue right away!"

"Where are you?"

"Stockji Glacier."

"Stockjigletscher?"

"Yes. Exactly."

Scott answers a few more questions and gets some instructions. "Most importantly," the woman tells him calmly and professionally, "do not approach the hole in the snow." As much as he would like to crawl over and yell down to his friend, the danger of more snow collapsing is just too great.

Even after making contact with people who might be able to help, Scott feels panicked and impotent. And alone. He looks up at the sky, his heart pounding with dread. The heli base, wherever it is, cannot be very close. He and his friend are in the middle of nowhere. Not knowing what else to do, he takes off his skis and sits down in the snow. Then he looks over to the hole. His friend is down there somewhere. How deep? Is he even still alive?

After the most awful fifteen minutes of his life, Scott finally hears the rapid *thwock-thwock-thwock* of an Airbus H130's rotor blades slicing through the light alpine air. And then he sees the most welcome sight he could ever imagine: a red helicopter soaring up over the horizon.

The pilot doesn't circle the site; likely having no problem spotting Scott on the white surface of the glacier, he comes directly toward him. He flies in low and hovers, never letting the copter's skis even touch the snow. Once in position, the door flies open and three men jump out next to Scott, all in red jumpsuits, goggles, helmets, and headphones. They move with confidence, wielding black duffels and a titanium rescue litter.

As quickly as it arrived, the helicopter departs. The rescuers wait until the rotors' noise and wash die down, then they move in close. They ask Scott a series of questions in accented English, soaking up as much information as possible, as quickly as possible. Then they get to work. Climbing harness already on, one of the men clips onto a rope by carabiner. He gets down on his belly, inches toward the hole through which Sean fell, then peers down.

"I've got a visual on the patient. Maybe twenty meters down," he relays to his partners. The man then yells down into the darkness. "We are here to help you. Sean, can you hear me?" Hearing nothing, he turns back to his team. *"Patient isch nöd asprächbar"* ("Patient is nonresponsive").

The other men are already busy erecting an aluminum tripod over the hole. When it's up, the rescuer with the harness, who it turns out is the mountain rescue specialist, eases down into the void. Another rescuer works the pulley system, lowering his teammate into the dark.

"Hallo? Hallo?" the rescuer shouts as he descends. It is slow going, but he finally settles just above Sean, one crampon digging into each opposite wall, headlamp illuminating Sean's crumpled body. The rescuer reaches down and gives him a few gentle but stiff nudges. "Can you hear me?"

Sean comes to, but his eyes take a few seconds to focus. He looks around in the half-light, trying to find the source of the disturbance. He locks on a man in red with a kind face.

"We're here to help. We're going to get you out of here."

The rescuer steps down onto the ledge. He works to chop Sean free from where he's wedged into the ice. The warmth of his body helps. Sean has melted the ice slightly. If he'd been down here much longer, his body temperature would have begun to drop, and that bit of water would have refrozen, making the rescue much more difficult. Victims of crevasse falls who aren't rescued quickly usually become entombed.

Once the specialist has Sean free, he slips a simple rescue harness around him, trying to move his body as little as possible. He clips the ends of the harness into his carabiner and radios the paramedic that they're ready to come up. Both men feel the ropes tighten, and they begin their slow hoist, which becomes excruciating for Sean. Everything hurts.

"I've got you, my friend."

"Thank you. *Thank you so much,*" Sean whispers through the agony as they inch closer to daylight.

Forty minutes later, Sean is safe and sound and warming up in an emergency room seventy miles away at the University Hospital in Bern, Switzerland. He's treated for a concussion, two broken ribs, a dislocated shoulder, and various cuts and bruises. But thanks to his rescuers, he is sure to make a full and fast recovery.

An emergency doctor, patient, and paramedic hang outside an Air Zermatt Eurocopter EC 135 helicopter during a rescue mission in the Swiss canton of Valais

In late 1946, eighteen months after the Nazi High Command surrendered in World War II, the Allied Forces were still mopping up and making sense of the new power structure in Europe. On November 19, eight passengers and four crew members boarded a Douglas C-53 Skytrooper in Vienna, Austria, and took off over the Alps, headed for Pisa, Italy. But terrible weather struck the mountains that day. The pilots became disoriented in the harsh conditions and had to crash-land on the Gauli Glacier in the Berner Oberland region of Switzerland—some fifty miles northeast of the Stockji Glacier.

Over subsequent days, radio operators at nearby airports triangulated the plane's rough position from the crew's emergency radio transmissions. Once British Royal Air Force and Swiss Air Force crews confirmed that location and pinpointed the crash site from high overhead, the Swiss military initiated a large-scale search-and-rescue operation.

On November 23, four days after the crash, after a thirteen-hour climb on skis, two Swiss soldiers reached the downed aircraft. The soldiers helped twelve survivors reach the Gauli Hut, another one of the Swiss Alpine Club's refuges.

The next day, two Swiss Air Force pilots, Captain Victor Hug and Major Pista Hitz, became alpine rescue legends when they managed to land two Fieseler Storch airplanes on the surface of the Gauli Glacier. The Storch was a rugged two-seater capable of making short-distance landings and takeoffs. Hug and Hitz rescued all the crash survivors, making eight trips down the mountain.

REMAINS OF A PRATT & WHITNEY R-1830 TWIN
WASP ENGINE FROM THE US C-53 SKYTROOPER THAT
CRASHED-LANDED ON GAULI GLACIER IN 1946

While air rescue in the Alps was born that day in 1946, it grew by fits and starts thereafter. Today, it's coordinated by a set of highly professional outfits: Air Zermatt, which covers the Upper Valais region of Switzerland; Air-Glaciers, which covers the Lower Valais; Rega, which covers the rest of Switzerland; the Peloton de Gendarmerie de Haute Montagne (PGHM) in France; and the Corpo Nazionale Soccorso Alpino e Speleologico (CNSAS) in Italy.

Employing more than fifteen hundred men and women—pilots, paramedics, flight physicians, mountain rescue specialists, and administrative staff at sixty bases and stations—these companies work together to provide passionate, committed, expert search-and-rescue (SAR) and helicopter emergency medical services (HEMS). In 2019 alone, they collectively performed well over twenty thousand mountain rescues.[1]

The areas and conditions in which these men and women work—with high altitudes, thin air, unforgiving terrain, fierce winds, low visibility—push their teams and helicopters to the very limits of endurance and performance. But these folks are the best in the world. The best pilots. The best mountaineers. The best doctors. State-of-the-art equipment. Constant training.

Alpine SAR and HEMS teams are on call 24 hours a day, 365 days a year. Anyone can be saved in mere minutes, almost anywhere in the Alps, with just the push of a button on a mobile phone. It doesn't matter where you come from or what problem you've gotten yourself into, these courageous men and women will go out and get you. Even in darkness, even in weather so bad that the helicopters can't fly, the teams still go out—on foot.

"We will never give up," said Gerold Biner, pilot and CEO of Air Zermatt. "If people need us, we will be here."[2]

Zermatt, Switzerland

Stockji Glacier Crevasse

Chamonix, France

Glacier Haute Route
Western Alps

MAX ELEVATION: 11,706 FEET
ASCENT / DESCENT: 27,516 / 32,110 FEET
DISTANCE: 114 MILES

BELiEF:
THINGS AREN'T SO BAD.

Do you ever think, *What's the big deal? Things are a mess, but so what? It's never good to dwell on the bad. Just get through the day. That's what's important. I mean, everyone's got broken relationships. Some addictions. A bit of chronic sin. Everyone's busy and weary, anxious and lonely. It's not like anyone can do anything about it. It's not like anyone can help. It's just what being a man looks like today.*

This kind of thinking is rooted neither in truth nor in the goodness of God. *Think again.*

Picture a world where everyone around you is kind, caring, encouraging, and willing to help when you need help. *Everyone.* Spouses, family members, friends, acquaintances, colleagues, bosses, political leaders, presidents. They are *for* you. Picture a world where people are quick to try to understand, quick to apologize, and quick to forgive.

Imagine that everyone around you is healthy and thriving, fully who God made them to be, passionate about their work but with plenty of time for rest and fellowship and celebration. Imagine a world where people love God, where everyone is confident and pleased with who they are and each person works hard to love the people around them.

Brother, we don't live in that kind of world.

We will. Rest assured, it's coming. But our world today is quite a bit different.

There's a darkness upon the earth. Think of the corruption. The atrocities. The hatred. The competition. The selfish cruelty. The callous brutality. All the killing. All the lying. All the godlessness. There is so much of it today that it's impossible to even take its measure. Things have simply stopped making sense.

"The world has gone completely mad," wrote gospel torchbearer John Eldredge.[3] The details are different, but we are all hurting and hard-pressed. These are difficult days—days of fear and heartache and pain, natural disasters and injustice, disease and deceit, loneliness and longing.

And yet, this racking pain isn't new. When God sent his Son into this world of ours more than two thousand years ago, what Jesus found was a people who were a lot like us. He found a world in crisis.

After Malachi, the last of the Old Testament prophets, God's voice fell silent for centuries. Henry Ironside, a preacher and theologian who pastored Moody Church in Chicago from 1929 to 1948, described that ancient period as a "troublous time." "The voice of inspiration," he wrote, "had ceased."[4] After Malachi, the Jewish people were left without a prophetic voice. And that lasted for four centuries—four hundred years of silence.

Without someone to speak truth and tell of God's love, the people of Judea, Samaria, Galilee, and the surrounding regions fell into a long night of confusion and doubt. God's people, Ironside wrote, were "harassed and distressed."[5] They devolved into quarreling sects, each claiming authority to interpret Scripture. And these sects drifted from God. Some became self-righteous and hypocritical, more interested in rules and rituals; others became aloof and unbelieving, more interested in power and worldly pleasures.

Sitting atop these factions sat two levels of government: a Jewish ruler under Roman imperial control. Opinions at every level differed about religion and taxes, and political disputes often got dirty and bloody. There were riots and revolts, intrigues and assassinations, persecution and enslavement, wars and rumors of war.

Jesus twice used the book of Isaiah to describe what he saw: "people dwelling in darkness," he said—people made needy and held captive and brokenhearted by the sin of the world (Luke 4:16–21; Isa. 61:1–2; Matt. 4:12–16; Isa. 9:1–2). In his Sermon on the Mount, he elaborated further. He spoke about what he encountered:

- People struggling with integrity and consistency; people struggling to do right and help each other, to serve and give when no one is watching; people struggling with lust and sexual immorality, with greed and selfishness, with envy and putting too much importance on money and work, possessions and material achievement (Matt. 5:27–30; 6:1–8; 6:16–34).

- People struggling with anger and cruelty, callousness and self-centeredness; people struggling with a lack of empathy for their fellow humans, a lack of mercy and care, especially toward people who are hard to love because they act or believe or look different (Matt. 5:21–22; 5:42–48; 6:1–4; 7:12).

- People struggling with honesty and authenticity; people struggling with a willingness to admit and own their failures, to apologize and make amends for their sins; people struggling with blame and judgment, with unforgiveness, stubbornness, holding grudges, and getting revenge (Matt. 5:23–26; 5:33–41; 6:14–15; 7:1–5).

- People struggling with misplaced fear, with an unhealthy fear of the future, with fear that they will have enough wealth, enough security and comfort; people struggling with trusting God—trusting he will provide for them, somehow (Matt. 6:25–34; 7:7–11).

- People struggling with making time for God; people struggling with making time to experience him and know him, with slowing down and listening for his voice; people struggling with trusting Jesus and basing their lives on his teaching (Matt. 7:21–27).

Jesus wasn't just describing a people of a bygone age; he was describing me. He was describing you, my brother. That very same darkness that enveloped and oppressed our first-century forebears now oppresses us two millennia later. Their "present darkness" is *our* present darkness (Eph. 6:12). Paul wrote about how creation was "subjected to futility" and how it remains in "bondage to corruption" (Rom. 8:20–21). He wrote about how the whole of creation was "groaning" (Rom. 8:22). Well, it groans still.

This darkness is not physical, of course. It's spiritual. The apostle Paul explained, it's imposed by the "rulers … authorities … cosmic powers … [and] spiritual forces of evil in the heavenly places" (Eph. 6:12). And it is enforced by "the power of Satan" (Acts 26:18).

Our collective curse—the curse of all ages since the Fall of Man— is that the "whole world lies in the power of the evil one" (1 John 5:19). An enemy rules this world, an enemy who wants only to "steal and kill and destroy" (John 10:10). An enemy who wants nothing more than to pillage and plunder our hearts, lives, and the entire world.

And he's doing just that. Even a cursory glance at the news on any given day confirms it.

- Another son overdoses on methamphetamines.
- Another daughter cuts herself due to overwhelming anxiety.
- Another mother is battered by her husband.
- Another grandmother is defrauded out of her life savings.
- Another officer is killed in the line of duty.
- Another father becomes addicted to fentanyl.
- Another niece is paralyzed by a drunk driver.
- Another sister is diagnosed with cancer.
- Another grandfather is lost to dementia.
- Another executive cheats on his wife of many years.
- Another athlete is molested by a trusted doctor.
- Another young man is shot by the police.
- Another soldier is killed by an IED in a far-off country.
- Another linebacker is diagnosed with severe brain trauma.
- Another pastor sexually harasses a young woman at work.
- Another CEO is fired and prosecuted for corporate fraud.
- Another politician covers up an appalling abuse of power.

Do you have experience with any of these things? How about anyone you love?

The facts and circumstances are different, but we're all treading in pitched and perilous circumstances—a world that's a far cry from the one we hope for and are made for. And whether we're willing to admit it or not, many of us have already fallen. We're hurting and have become trapped in the deep and dark and cold of this spiritual reality.

And most of us have been traveling alone and have no one to call out to. No one is on our speed dial. No one knows what peril we've gotten ourselves into. No one knows to mobilize a rescue mission.

This murky landscape is our common predicament. We live among crooks and cowards, authoritarians and abusers—but none of us is innocent either. We "all have sinned and fall short of the glory of God" (Rom. 3:23). We "all stumble in many ways" (James 3:2). Paul and James didn't use the word "all" lightly. "All" means *all*. We *all* contribute to this "present evil age" (Gal. 1:4). We're complicit in trespasses and transgressions because of our sin.

Evil seduces and persuades, accuses and torments. But it's you and I who *act*. Dark forces operate in the spiritual realm; we physical beings operate in this material world. They tempt and urge evil, encouraging our baser inclinations: "the desires of the flesh" (1 John 2:16). But it's *we* who execute that evil. It is we, my friend, who treat our brothers and sisters carelessly, maliciously, exploitatively. "O faithless and twisted generation" (Matt. 17:17). Were it not for us, all this sorrow wouldn't exist—for the corrupt cosmic powers would have no corporal being to influence.

But we are here; we are influenced. And Paul described for Timothy what it looks like for people to live under these infernal influences:

> People will be lovers of self, lovers of money, proud, arrogant, abusive, disobedient to their parents,

ungrateful, unholy, heartless, unappeasable, slan-
derous, without self-control, brutal, not loving
good, treacherous, reckless, swollen with conceit,
lovers of pleasure rather than lovers of God, having
the appearance of godliness, but denying its power.
(2 Tim. 3:2–5)

Paul could have been describing our day. This hour. *Right now.*

This is a story that goes further back than merely two thousand years.
Very long ago, in the extravagance of the Garden of Eden, near the
dawn of human existence itself, a shadow crept over the land. The
enemy probed and probed again, looking for vulnerabilities. And then
he found one: the human heart. Satan coaxed and cajoled, tempting
Adam and Eve to rebel against God. The serpent challenged and lied
and tried to lead them astray. And when they went that way, everything
changed. A darkness descended over the whole earth.

That darkness is our darkness now. Somehow, Adam's rebellion
became our own. "By the one man's disobedience the many were made
sinners" (Rom. 5:19). Sin and rebellion gained access into our personalities and bodies. Disease and death did too. Darkness poured into our
hearts, blackening them toward God. We lost our ease and innocence,
our devotion and connection to him. No longer were we able to draw
as near to him because he dwells in light that had become, for us,
"unapproachable" (1 Tim. 6:16).

Darkness blackened our hearts toward each other too. "To the
woman he said … 'Your desire shall be contrary to your husband, but
he shall rule over you'" (Gen. 3:16). Strife arose between Adam and
Eve—the only humans then in existence—foreshadowing the strife
that exists now among and between all humans and has throughout
our history. Foreshadowing malice and murder, betrayal and abuse,
intolerance and inequity, contempt and competitiveness.

Darkness even blackened our hearts toward ourselves. We lost wholeness, self-confidence, unselfconsciousness. It's why we struggle for self-awareness and do self-destructive things. It's why we sabotage relationships, careers, bodies, and our mental well-being with unwise addictions, unhelpful habits, and unhealthy relationships.

And finally, darkness blackened our hearts toward the physical world. We stopped caring for our home, ceased living in harmony with it. Darkness overtook it too. "The world we live in, with its cyclones, tornadoes, tempests, tidal waves and other forces of destruction, is under occupation," wrote the truth-seeking, truth-telling A. W. Tozer.[6] Creation became impure and infirm, sullied and stained, hard and dangerous—full of "thorns and thistles" (Gen. 3:18).

"The days," wrote Paul, "are evil" (Eph. 5:3–16).

One insidious aspect of the darkness surrounding us is that it makes us blind (1 John 2:11). *The darkness makes us blind to the darkness.* We get used to it, distracted and lulled into complacency. We become numb and hardened to the scale and scope of the menace. (I sure was.)

The dark makes us behave as if we are drunk or asleep or even dead (1 Thess. 5:5–8; Eph. 5:3–16). We become unseeing, uncaring, confused, and aimless. "The one who walks in the darkness does not know where he is going" (John 12:35). We become casual toward sin, neglectful toward love, hard-hearted toward others' plights, and lax toward self-care and soul care.

And then, and then, dark voices offer help. They whisper, suggesting that our problems can be solved by devoting more hours to work, or by putting more money into our bank accounts, or by distraction and escape, or bitterness and isolation. They lure us to self-medicate with work, food, sex, pornography, gambling, alcohol, prescription painkillers, and illicit drugs.

Of course, these dark solutions are only meant to take us deeper into the darkness. They cause new and improved problems or exacerbate existing ones. And then a new message is whispered in the shadows: *Get used to it. Don't worry so much.* The darkness lulls us into complacency: *This is just how things are. This is how the world is.* The night sings us back to sleep: *This is who you are. None of this is going to change.*

And we lose heart. We put our heads down. We grind. Going nowhere. Rather than getting better, we settle for getting by. Rather than overcoming sin, moving beyond it, beyond unhealthy habits, escaping unhealthy relationships, we simply narrow our lives and try to get used to the dark, to endure the pain and dislocation. We settle for *stuck* and *lost* and *empty.* We manage our pain. We survive the day, but just barely.

We become imposters too, hiding our deep needs and dark deeds, obscuring our problems rather than dealing with them. Instead of learning how to hurt other people less—and ourselves too—we isolate. We become workaholics. Heavy drinkers. Porn addicts. Exhausted insomniacs.

And when anyone asks how we're doing, it's "Things are good. Thanks for asking."

Desperate ambition. Desperate anger. Desperate addiction. Desperate sin.

Quiet men, desperate for rescue.

In the days before the Last Supper, prior to his death and resurrection, Jesus rode into Jerusalem, and the people hailed his entry. "Hosanna in the highest!" (Matt. 21:1–11; Mark 11:1–11; John 12:12–15). *Hosanna* is a Greek word meaning "save, we pray" or "oh, save now!" or "please save!"[7] The shouts echoed the groans of all creation.

And that was exactly why Jesus was there. He felt our hearts aching, and his heart hurt too. So he came with urgency and purpose and overwhelming might. He brought the cavalry. *He led the charge.* He came to "rescue us from the present evil age" (Gal. 1:4).[8] "I am the light of the world. Whoever follows me will not walk in darkness, but will have the light of life" (John 8:12).

"For God did not send his Son into the world to
condemn the world, but in order that the world
might be saved through him." —John the apostle

Three words used in the original Greek New Testament are
instructive here. The word *sōzō* means to "deliver out of danger and
into safety."[9] It appears more than one hundred times in Scripture.
Both *iaomai* and *therapeuō* mean "to heal," and in aggregate, they
appear about seventy times.[10] These words express what Jesus is all
about: rescuing us from our sin and the sin of the world, healing us,
restoring us. Physically. Emotionally. Spiritually.

When the righteous and devout prophet Simeon first laid his
eyes on the infant Jesus, he rejoiced to God the Father and said, "My
eyes have seen your salvation" (Luke 2:25–32). Jesus *is* our salvation.
Standing in eternity, full of outrageous love, God the Father sees and
understands everything. He knows our inky plights. He knows what
we need most. And he knew just the man for the rescue mission.

Nothing is too horrible or dangerous for Jesus. He can handle
the worst of the worst. And the darkness doesn't stand a chance. The
forces of darkness couldn't detain or delay him. He flashed into hell
itself and defeated them on their own ground. He brought light. He
brought resurrection power. He brought creation power—the very
power that created *everything everywhere*. He faced down sin and death
and vanquished them both. His love and mercy were and are simply
too powerful.

"The Life-Light blazed out of the darkness; the darkness couldn't
put it out (John 1:3–5).[11] He rescued us then; he rescues us now. He
saves us from each other, from ourselves, and from this dark world.
He comes to bring us "out of darkness into his marvelous light"
(1 Pet. 2:9).

He will do anything to reach you. Jesus will climb the highest
mountain. Cross the most treacherous sea. Endure the most forbidding
desert. Invade the darkest forest. He'll never stop coming. He'll even
die for you. *He did that already.*

And he's the only one who can. Only he can stand against the darkness. By ourselves, we are grossly unprepared, undertrained, and ill-equipped. The night is just too black, too leaden. And it stretches over all of us. Our intentions for renewed effort, for discovering new self-help insight, for executing on sage advice, they won't do it. Not even close.

Only Jesus. And he is coming. *He is here.*

If you're in the midst of a major crisis or just living in a world in crisis, here's my news for you: You are found. The cavalry has arrived.

The safety net of the ancient world was the family, immediate and extended. It was the kinship system. The clan. The tribe. The village. This was certainly true in Judea at the time of Jesus' life. To survive those troubled times, people gathered together and relied on one another. They relied on parents. Siblings. Aunts and uncles. All manner of cousins and close friends.

Family units were a person's support network. Those flesh-and-blood groups met physical, emotional, and spiritual needs. They provided for basic physical and material well-being. They offered protection from dangers, both human and natural; a sense of belonging; and a layer of accountability.

It wasn't a perfect system, of course. But it was much better than braving the adversity alone.

When Jesus arrived, though, everything changed. His ability to love and care far exceeded anything any human system could ever provide—even the strongest of families. Jesus came as a supercharged, supernatural need-meeter. He gave people who were hurting what they so desperately required: a fresh start, a second chance, renewed joy and vigor and peace. Salvation.

People who came into contact with Jesus got to experience up-close how *God* keeps people safe. They got to see with their own eyes the way God loves, the way God cares. God became physical and personal; they could reach out and touch him. They could hear his actual voice. And they came away changed. With new energy and strength and faith. With hearts burning with love.

For Peter's mother-in-law, for Bartimaeus, for the man who was blind at Bethsaida, for the man who was disabled at Bethesda, for the men with leprosy, Jesus wasn't an idea. For Mary Magdalene, for the Samaritan woman at Jacob's well, for Zacchaeus, for the woman caught in adultery, for the sinful woman who anointed Jesus' feet with ointment, Jesus wasn't distant. He was a man. But he was God too. He was an up-close and fantastic miracle. He was the ultimate rescuer, and he was right there in front of them—right *in* their physical circumstances.

And people came in droves. Desperate for rescue, they got what they needed.

But his time was so short. After his crucifixion, death, and resurrection, in a town about a mile and a half east of Jerusalem, on the southeastern slope of the Mount of Olives, Jesus prayed a blessing over his disciples and then "parted from them and was carried up into heaven" (Luke 24:51).

He was gone.

For his followers, for those saved and healed—and those who desperately wanted to be—it must have been incredibly confusing. *Are we on our own again? Are we going back to how it was before? Are the miracles over? No more rescue?*

But he'd been preparing those same followers all along, and they were now ready—whether they knew it or not. Before he left, he assured them that his leaving wasn't a bad thing. In fact, he said it was *good*. Good for all of us. It was better than if he were to stay and continue what he had been doing. He said, "If I do not go away, the Helper will not come to you. But if I go, I will send him to you" (John 16:7).

Two years earlier, probably in the springtime, Jesus was in northern Israel, in Galilee, teaching and healing. People thronged to this man who brought freedom and restoration and hope. On one occasion, so many people showed up that he and his twelve disciples weren't even able to eat. They packed so tightly into a house that all Jesus could do was teach. (Being him, he also managed to heal a man.)

At some point, the crowd passed word to Jesus that his mother and brothers were outside. Because of the crush, his family couldn't enter but still wanted to speak with him. I can imagine that those who brought the message did so with urgency, likely expecting Jesus to go out to them at once or have them brought in. He did neither.

> And a crowd was sitting around him, and they said to him, "Your mother and your brothers are outside, seeking you." And he answered them, "Who are my mother and my brothers?" And looking about at those who sat around him, he said, "Here are my mother and my brothers! For whoever does the will of God, he is my brother and sister and mother." (Mark 3:32–35)

Why did he say that? Well, he was teaching his followers (and us) about something new. Something astonishing. He was teaching them about a whole new *kind* of family. He took the idea of family to an entirely different place and a wholly new level.

That knowing Northumbrian N. T. Wright called it an "alternative family."[12] It's a supercharged support structure. A supernaturally strong safety net.

It's important to note that Jesus wasn't renouncing his natural family, and he wasn't teaching us to do that either. From Genesis and Exodus, through Proverbs and Psalms, and into the New Testament, Scripture teaches us to love and honor and care for our natural families (see Gen. 2:24; Ex. 20:12; Prov. 11:29; 15:20; 22:6; Ps. 127:3–5; 128:3; Eph. 5:22–33; Col. 3:18–21; 1 Tim. 5:8). What he was teaching us is that this new family is better. *Much* better. More significant, more substantial, and much better equipped to meet our human needs.

Jesus promised that this new family made up of his followers would be a hundred times better than any existing family. He promised Peter that he would receive a "hundredfold" increase in "houses and brothers and sisters and mothers and children and lands" (Mark 10:29–30). He wasn't making a promise about affluence, not worldly affluence, at least. He was making a promise about love and care and protection. That's what "houses and brothers and sisters and mothers and children and lands" did back then. They met human needs.

That is the power of Christian community, *and it's available now*. Anyone and everyone gets to be a part of it *now*—if we want it. Jesus promised this one-hundred-times increase both "in the age to come" *and* "now in this time" (Mark 10:29–30). That's precisely why Lieutenant Cummings was willing to lay down his life in order to bring companionship and community to the men of the US Army Forces in the Far East.

Notice that one thing Jesus doesn't mention is fathers: "houses and brothers and sisters and mothers and children and lands" (Mark 10:30). This is simply and beautifully because God himself is part of all of this. *He's* the father of this new family. He's the head of this new kinship system. "And call no man your father on earth, for you have one Father, who is in heaven" (Matt. 23:9).

And it's not only him. Jesus and the Holy Spirit are involved too, and just as deeply.

This is the support network of the ancient family but turned up to a hundred. This is the Mediterranean clan but overflowing with the Father's love, under the noble rule of Jesus, animated with the most potent force in the universe—the power that created stars and planets, humans and every living thing, the power that conquered sin and death.

Prior to this, Jesus was the highest concentration of God's presence on earth. But now *you* are, my friend. I am too. *That* was Lieutenant Cummings's secret. God is God, and we are not, of course. But his power and brilliance and love dwell *within* us, within these earthen vessels. And so, what Cummings knew was that God comes to each of us *through* our friends. Here again are the chaplain's words as they echoed off the steel walls of that dark and dank Japanese prison ship: "Believe in yourselves and in the goodness of one another. Know that in yourselves and in those that stand near you, you see the image of God."[13]

Cummings didn't actually die in the darkness; he died in the light. He died right next to his Father. Beside his King. In the midst of that brutal war and the blackness of that prison hold, he remained in God's marvelous light the entire time because he was with his beloved brothers right to the end.

Jesus will never leave you nor forsake you. He will never let you down. Sometimes it may seem like he does. But he doesn't. Ever. If it ever appears as though he's let you down, it's simply because you and I can't see things from his perspective. He is always there for us, interested and caring and engaged. And through this family, this *army*, he has time for everyone. The Spirit of God is no longer contained in just one man. He dwells inside a multitude of men and women. "Behold," Jesus said, "the kingdom of God is in the midst of you" (Luke 17:21). He's everywhere, able to help anyone and everyone who wants it.

God sent Jesus to rescue us again and again but mostly *through* his people. Mostly through our Christian brothers and sisters. Mostly through those unlikely family members, those quirky friends, overlooked acquaintances, those surprising strangers—the people who surround us, supercharged with his love. "God comes to us in the midst of our human need, and the most pressing needs of our time demand community in response," wrote Parker Palmer.[14] At this hour on the earth, he gives *us* "power" to care for each other's "bruised and hurt lives" (Matt. 10:1).[15]

This family is indeed an army, but unlike any this world has ever seen. It's fearsome, but only against the darkness. "For the weapons of our warfare are not of the flesh but have divine power to destroy strongholds" (2 Cor. 10:4). This army is quick and clever and massively strong—an army of love. It's an army that brings freedom to those of us who are captive, aid to those of us who are sick, truth to those of us who are confused, healing to those of us who are hurt.

Whenever Jesus performs a miracle, it's inherently and infinitely mysterious. Again, he is God, and we are not. From our perspective, his miraculous rescues are uncontrollable and unpredictable. But that's not *entirely* true, and community is a good example of why. The miracles that happen in community are, on some level, quite predictable indeed.

Jesus promised that he's uniquely present when we gather in community. "For where two or three are gathered in my name, there am I among them" (Matt. 18:20). When Jesus said these words, he was perhaps explaining how to restore relationships that had broken, but it's just as true in every other context too. Jesus is uniquely present when his followers gather because he is uniquely present in each of his followers' hearts. His very Spirit dwells there.

So if we ever want to encounter the supernatural, he's told us exactly what to do: *gather.* "No one has ever seen God," wrote John the apostle (1 John 4:12). But when two or three brothers gather, we get to *experience* him—"if we love one another, God abides in us and his love is perfected in us" (1 John 4:12). When two or three brothers gather, heaven and earth collide. God and man interact.

"When I go to my brother," wrote the brilliant minister and mutineer Dietrich Bonhoeffer, "I am going to God."[16] When two or three brothers gather, we encounter the genuine and miraculous presence of God himself. And we see miracles happen.

We won't know when or where, but we never need to wait long. The specifics of the miracles are unpredictable, but the fact that rescue will happen at some point is inevitable. Men will find acceptance and belonging. Wholeness and wholesomeness. Men will get free from lies. From unhealthy attachments. From unhelpful beliefs about God and themselves. Men will get free from substances and circumstances and sins from which they never thought they'd get free. Men will discover peace and joy, rest and optimism. They will find a God they never dreamed actually existed.

We can, therefore, breathe a sigh of relief and finally accept Jesus' commands: "Fear not"; "Do not be anxious about your life, what you will eat or what you will drink, nor about your body, what you will put on"; "Do not be anxious about tomorrow" (Matt. 10:31; 6:25; 6:34). We don't need to fear anything, because we are full members in good standing in his transcendentally fearsome surrogate family. And this family has got our backs.

What does this kind of community look like in the life of a man? Because of our human limitations, we cannot be in direct community with every follower of Jesus in the world. Being in authentic community takes a commitment of time and energy, and we are finite beings with only so much of both. We can, therefore, only reasonably expect to be in close community with a handful of men.

But having these few men is essential. And these men become our rescue teams.

When we have a rescue team, we never again have to trudge and struggle across this landscape alone. We have brothers to make sure we're never left behind. To give us hope when ours wanes. To give us strength when ours flags. We have brothers to encourage and counsel and challenge us, celebrate and grieve with us, help us see what we cannot, speak truth when we need truth, and guide us into God-given identity. And we can do the very same for them, right back.

The most amazing part, though, is that when the men of a rescue team come for one of their brothers, it's not just them. It's God too.

God Almighty. The God of the Universe *in* them. That's why authentic Christian community can be a hundred times better than anything else. A friend showing up in a time of need is awesome. A friend *and* God showing up is biblical.

When we have a rescue team, we can engage this dark world alongside an elite force filled with Holy Spirit fire. And this is what we need. More than dollars in any bank account. More than any achievement or recognition. More than any sexual conquest. More than pornography. More than alcohol. More than food. More than anything this world can offer.

Beyond the ultramodern helicopters, alpine rescuers carry loads of advanced equipment. They bring cables, ropes, harnesses, pulleys, carabiners, nuts and cams, ice axes, rescue bags, rescue nets for lifting victims, litters, slings, splints, braces, medical kits, radios, GPS devices, and all manner of other tools.

An Air Zermatt mountain rescue technician being lowered into a crevasse near Breithorn mountain in Zermatt, Switzerland

But when we rescue our brothers, our friends, our family members from the darkness of this world—or when they save us—we don't need any special gear or special training. "*You* are the equipment," Jesus explained (Matt.10:9–10).[17] We have everything we need already. We have our Father God, willing to pour so much love into our lives that it overflows onto our loved ones. We have the Holy Spirit in our hearts, guiding us with the right words and the most helpful actions. And we have Jesus, who is always there to redeem things when we get it wrong and make mistakes.

And so, whenever we relent and start taking even simple actions toward brotherhood, whenever we agree to meet even one or two guys for coffee or breakfast or whatever and begin engaging in some kind of authentic community, we begin participating in something beyond anything we can see with our eyes—certainly beyond anything we've been taught to expect. Those moments become momentous, red-chopper-speeding-up-over-the-horizon occasions.

This is how it should be—every man having a band of brothers. It's how we become strong and resilient. Not alone, but together. *United.* It's how we meet problems head-on. It's how we overcome them.

When we find our rescue teams, we can come out of isolation and loneliness and find true friendship and fellowship. We can be welcomed and known and understood. We can find safe places—where we belong, where we can be ourselves and be accepted just as we are. We can find places of honesty and accountability. Places where we can finally confront our wounds, our demons, the lies we believe. Where we can be lifted up out of sin and rebellion.

When we find our teams, we get unstuck. We find places where we can grow. We find people willing to walk with us and talk with us. People with whom we can share our burdens and from whom we can get help when we stumble or when life knocks us down. We find people willing to stand in the gap and even provide for basic needs in challenging times.

When we find our teams, we find God too. We find places where we can encounter more of his love. Places where we can sense the presence and movements of the Holy Spirit. Where we can see signs of Jesus—and wonders.

When we find our teams, we find ourselves. We become able to become the men we're meant to become: rugged and mature, wise and kind, gentle and generous. And we become men fit and ready to rescue others, because we've been rescued ourselves.

How does that sound? Do you want to find *your* rescue team?

Larry Crabb, a formidable figure in Christian counseling, wrote about something he imagined one time in prayer:

> As I prayed this morning for a friend going through rough times, an image formed in my mind. I saw a Gibraltar-size rock emerging out of a wild ocean. As the rock took its place, steady, solid, and thoroughly settled, I could see frightened people floundering in the water looking to the rock and finding hope.[18]

"The community of God's people," wrote Crabb, "is that rock in stormy seas, an island of peace in a world of pain."[19]

Life is hard and unforgiving, and we're weary. But Jesus will send out an army whenever we want it. He'll lead a rescue operation, right into the darkest, the loneliest places. Even into the scariest moments of our lives.

Brother, we *can* call in the cavalry. But if you're curious why you rarely, if ever, hit that button, just keep reading. That's what we're going to explore in the next chapter.

– CLIP IN –
"FOUND"
002

We lost our way long ago. Generation upon generation, we've been crying out for rescue. A mass of humanity. A multitude of voices, hurting and lost. Each of us in our own lands, in our own languages. In our own ways. Knowing and unknowing. We've cried out, "Hosanna!" Save us from the darkness. Save us from each other. Save us from ourselves.

And God heard our cries. He came for us. Jesus came running. He brought rescue. Then he formed a rescuing army. It all started with him—with one man. But now, his Holy Spirit–filled army numbers in the billions. And if we want it, brother, we can be found. If we want it, we can be rescued.

If we want it, we can find revitalized lives and reinvigorated faith. And our hearts can be changed. Our relationships with God can change. We can become closer. Our relationships with other people can change. We can become more loving. Our relationships with ourselves can change. We can become kinder. And our relationships with the darkness can change too. We can become much less susceptible to its evil clutches.

So what do you think?

Consider this question and capture your response in a journal or a notes app.

002.1   What struck you about this chapter or in the story of the alpine rescue? Pull out a pen or pencil or your phone and describe whatever stood out to you personally.

002.2   How convinced are you that this evil and enveloping darkness exists? That our world "lies in the power of the evil one" (1 John 5:19)? Circle a number below:

<< I JUST DON'T SEE IT - - - - - - - - - - - - - - - - - - I SEE IT EVERY DAY >>
1   2   3   4   5   6   7   8   9   10

Whatever number you've chosen, write a short paragraph or two explaining your answer.

Engage in an experiment. Open up today's newspaper or the news app on your phone. Take a few minutes to skim the articles. Then look again. Look *through* the news stories. Underneath them. What do you sense? What do you see? People thriving? People hurting? People filled with joy and hope? People filled with fear and pain?

Now, choose one article. Select the one that touched your heart the most, and pray for the people involved. Ask Jesus to come for the people in the story, the victims and villains both. Ask Jesus to bring miraculous restoration into whatever situation your news story describes.

Would you be willing to commit to praying this same prayer for these same people for one week?

Consider these questions and capture your responses.

002.3   What's been your experience of the darkness? How have you personally experienced cruelty, rejection, deceit, pain, fear, anguish, loneliness, or despair? Choose two periods of your life (for example, childhood, adolescence, young adulthood, middle adulthood, late adulthood). Write a paragraph or two (or more) describing how the darkness of this world has affected you during these two periods.

002.4   How desperate are you right now? How much would you like
         to be rescued? Circle a number below:

<< I'm doing okay - Come now, Jesus! >>

   1   2   3   4   5   6   7   8   9   10

Write out a personal prayer. Be specific, and ask Jesus for precisely
what you need.

Then **pray**. Pray your prayer and this one too.

> *Jesus, tell me. I want to know. Are we stuck? Will
> things ever change? Can this fractured world ever heal?
> Can we, as a people, come together? And will I ever
> overcome these things that I've been fighting my entire
> life, inside myself and outside? Will I ever get free of
> these things that are tormenting me? Can things get
> better? Can I get better? Is any of this even possible?*
>
> *Open my eyes, Jesus. Open my heart. I want to
> know that you're real. I want to know that you're here
> and working. I want to know that rescue is possible. I
> want to trust you. Help me to see what you're doing in
> our world and in my life. Help me to see you.*
>
> *And please, promise me that everything's going to
> be okay—somehow, someway, someday.*
> *Amen.*

BETTER MAN

They say the measure of a man
Is that he's strong and never weak

But I couldn't break the chains I wore
It took a better Man than me

They say never let 'em see you cry
You gotta hide your troubles deep

To show me how to lay them down
It took a better man than me

// Stephen McWhirter, songwriter

HOISTS AND FINS AND FRATERNITY

Boreal seas have long tempted fishermen with the promise of riches—of waters teeming with fish. Of course, the cruel weather common to such remote places has caused even brave men to think twice about leaving more temperate and sensible latitudes behind.

Undaunted, more than four dozen boats plow northward. Tomorrow, they'll be prospecting for the prized red king crab on what the ancient Yup'ik peoples call *Imarpik* and what one antique western map calls the Sleepy Sea. It's a body of water and ice that sits high on the globe, above the Aleutian archipelago, between Alaska's mainland and Russia's Far East. Anything but sleepy, it's been known to the world as the Bering Sea ever since Danish navigator Vitus Bering first battled its harsh waves in 1728.

The F/V *Saint Elias*, steaming near the rear of the fleet, is a ninety-two-foot hunk of steel crewed by five indefatigable deckhands and one invariably irate captain. These men will spend the next two weeks hacking through freezing spray and howling winds, working eighteen-hour shifts dropping and picking up crab pots about five hundred miles west-southwest of their homeport of Kodiak, Alaska.

A crab pot is a seven-by-seven-by-three-foot, eight-hundred-pound metal cage. When crabs crawl into one, baited by herring, sardines, or codfish, it's a one-way trip. And the men belowdecks are praying that a lot crawl in. Larger boats carry upwards of two hundred pots on their decks. The *Saint Elias* is a smaller vessel, though; it holds only forty.

After baiting the pots, crab fishermen drop them to the ocean floor in straight lines or "strings," which makes retrieval easier. Captains target places where seas are about four hundred feet deep because that's where red king crab tend to congregate. When a string has been left for a time, crews circle back and pick up the cages, hoping they are chock-full.

The *Saint Elias* captain is steering toward a specific spot on the water, a pin on his chart, an area he's fished for decades—just as his father did before him. He'll reach these favored fishing grounds by morning, and then his crew will commence the frantic and exhausting on-deck disco of men and crab and flying steel.

When not dropping or pulling pots, the deckhands keep busy getting bait ready for the next string, cleaning the boat, cooking meals, changing oil, or making repairs to equipment or engines. It'll be a hectic twelve days.

Right now, though, Gabe Martinez is trying to get some sleep. Earlier, he and his fellow deckhands got caught up on everything that has happened in their lives since they were last together, and then they wolfed down a bunch of Hungry-Man frozen dinners. None of them talked about it, but this crew is a family. Sure, they sorely miss spouses and kids back home in the lower forty-eight, but it's good to be back on the water with old friends—*with brothers.*

Another topic of conversation during dinner was the grim overnight forecast. The National Weather Service has issued gale warnings: winds up to forty-five knots with heavy spray and seas to twenty-one feet. Freezing sea spray is dangerous for all vessels but particularly so for crab boats because it likes to grab on to all those crab pots stacked high on deck—making boats dangerously top-heavy with ice. Then again, this is a veteran crew, and no one's worried. Boats ice every winter; they deal with it.

Gabe tosses in his bunk, anxious that he won't be able to fall asleep but, at the same time, exceedingly grateful to have a few hours to rest up for the grueling work ahead. As he finally drifts off, the *Saint Elias* is already doomed. None of the men know it yet, but the boat will soon be resting upside down on the dark and sandy Bering seafloor.

It isn't one thing that seals the vessel's fate. It's a cascade of them. Weather is one. That ice forming up on deck is loading the ship with tons of extra weight, severely affecting its stability. Metal fatigue is another. As the boat crashes through wave after wave, a corroded and failing seacock valve is allowing seawater to seep then pour then gush into the engine room. But here's the biggie: the bilge alarm in the engine room has stopped working. It should be notifying the crew that water is accumulating in the compartment, but no one's checked it in some time.

Forty minutes pass, and then no one needs an alarm to know that the boat is in trouble. Ice on deck and flooding in the engine room join forces to make it impossible for the boat to right itself in the twenty-foot swells and waves. When Gabe wakes, the boat is listing so hard to starboard that he's very nearly standing straight up in his bunk. Dumbfounded for only an instant, Gabe reaches for the bed frame, then the floor and the walls. He struggles across his room—nearly sideways. As waves crash into the upturned hull and the boat lurches in unholy directions, Gabe grabs at his tumbling suitcase. He fumbles with the zipper, then finally rips it open. He yanks out a bulky red survival suit.

Just outside his cabin, he hears food stores and gear crashing. He hears the calls and curses of his mates—some near, some more faint. But he's focused on one thing right now: getting this blasted suit on. It's all that matters. That black water out there is barely above 40 degrees Fahrenheit, and he knows he's soon going to be in it. If he doesn't get his suit on, he's going to die.

Gabe smells engine smoke as he grapples with the suit, trying to jam his legs in while sliding down the floor toward starboard. Once he's more or less in, he turns his attention to getting his right arm into the proper hole. When he manages that, he yanks the contraption up over his shoulders and pulls the hood down over his head. Then he tries to snake his left arm back and into the remaining armhole. After three tries, he finally gets it in.

Now he just needs to zip up. But the built-in gloves are comically large. When he finally gets hold of the zipper lanyard through the thick neoprene, he pulls and pulls and pulls. Every time, the suit just bunches around his torso. He stops, takes a quick breath, then pulls again but with less force. The zipper finally moves, but this time it gets stuck on his T-shirt. And then the lights go out.

Instinctively, he lunges for the companionway. He slams his head into something, bangs his knee on something else. He hears his friends all around him but can't see much. Only flashes. He screams to his friends. "Get your survival suits on! Get out of the boat!" The galley is chaos. Gear and food and dishes and pots and two microwaves and a coffee maker crash around him as waves thrash the rolling-over boat.

Gabe fights through the chaos, getting knocked all over the small room. Still calling out to his dear friends as he goes, he finally reaches the gear room, scrambling, crawling, willing his way toward the exterior door. He slams into it, feeling for the dual handles that hold the door shut. He's opened this door hundreds of times, but not like this. He forces the handles to move, the door pops, and Gabe falls out.

He's operating on instinct now, and those instincts are shouting to him: *Get to the high side of the boat!* He clambers up the deck, crawls over the gunwales and onto the hull of the rolling vessel. He can't believe how loud it is: wind screaming, steel creaking and breaking, waves slamming into the boat from crazy angles. But his mind focuses on his two greatest enemies: drowning and hypothermia. Like every crab fisherman before him, he knows the best way to stay alive is to stay out of the water.

At this point, though, a swim is a foregone conclusion. This boat is going down, but he tries to put off the inevitable as long as he can. The ship continues to roll in the rough seas but seems to settle a bit when it's almost upside down. Gabe crouches, holding on to the wet hull as best he can, and he watches. Waves come closer and closer. Then, with one particularly large jolt, he loses his grip and begins sliding.

This is it.

Knowing he can't win the battle, he stops his desperate grasping at the slick metal and springs into the pitch-black water. Even in the survival suit, the cold water is bracing. Water trickles into the space between his body and the suit; he could never get it fully zipped. The cold speeds up his breathing, making him gulp for air. In his panic, he kicks away from the heaving boat.

But then another sensation grabs at his heart. He's getting *too* far away. That sinking hulk is his home. Without it, without his friends, he's going to be all alone in this vast expanse and the biting cold. But there's nothing he can do. The massive waves treat a 190-pound flailing and flesh-and-blood body differently than a 300-ton steel carcass, and the distance grows at a rate that sends terror through Gabe's chest.

And that's when he sees it. Fifteen yards away, he sees the EPIRB bobbing on the surface, antenna up, LED blinking. It brings a rush of hope. An emergency position-indicating radio beacon is a battery-powered radio transmitter. It sends distress signals and GPS coordinates to satellites operated by a consortium of rescue services. Mounted on a boat's exterior surface, these EPIRBs are made to deploy and float to the surface when they become submerged in ten or so feet of water. They offer the possibility, however slim in many cases, that rescuers might be able to find survivors within what's known as the "golden day"—the first twenty-four hours following an accident, during which survivors have the best chance of being rescued.

But Gabe soon loses sight of both the boat and the EPIRB. His visibility is so impaired by the darkness, the spray, the swells, that he doesn't know whether the ship's gone under or has just gotten too far away. Alone in the roiling water, Gabe begins to accept that death is very likely just moments away. He feels so small out there, and his thoughts turn dark.

Should I just suck some seawater in and get things over with? Or should I just wait for hypothermia to take me? At least I got my survival suit on. Someone will be able to find my floating body, and my family can have some closure.

Just then, a US Coast Guard rescue helicopter takes off from Dutch Harbor. The four-person crew—pilot, copilot, flight mechanic, rescue swimmer—has just dropped off equipment to a Coast Guard cutter docked there for repairs. Fuel tanks full, the helicopter is now on its way back to base: Air Station Kodiak.

Dutch Harbor is only about two hundred miles south of the position given by the *Saint Elias* EPIRB when the boat slid beneath the surface of the sea. And that mayday signal bounced around, office to office, and finally reached the Kodiak station. Kodiak wasted no time and radioed the heli crew—and the men don't hesitate. They bank their Sikorsky MH-60 Jayhawk left, tilt the airframe's nose over, and use those twin General Electric T700 turboshaft engines to drive right into the raging storm. The Jayhawk has a top speed of about two hundred miles per hour. In this hellacious weather, though, the pilots expect a 100-mph bronc ride.

About two hours later, the Jayhawk arrives on scene, but the crew sees only darkness. After a few long, tense minutes of straining, of surveying the ocean surface for any sign of survivors, the rescue team agrees on a search plan. They take their craft into a sweeping pattern, methodically scouring the black waves.

"I see a light!" yells the flight mechanic. "Two o'clock, three hundred yards!"

"Got it. Mark it, Ken."

"Roger that."

What the guys are seeing is a tiny but high-intensity LED light that's attached to Gabe's survival suit. Like the EPIRB, it automatically activated and began blinking when it came into contact with the Bering brine.

The pilot wheels his helicopter right, coming in low over the light.

Down on the surface, getting pummeled by twenty-foot seas and hammering winds, Gabe almost can't believe what he hears: the *thwut-thwut-thwut-thwut-thwut* of the Jayhawk's rotors beating the wind and rain.

As the helicopter drops in close, the pilot struggles to hold position overhead. The rotor spray gets so intense for Gabe, it feels like he's breathing needles. Through the darkness, though, Gabe sees an astonishing sight: a rescue swimmer descending on quarter-inch cable. The flight mechanic, crouched in the helicopter's door, moves the swimmer up and down, timing his moves with the surging seas. After several attempts, the swimmer drops into the water a few yards from Gabe.

Once in the water, the swimmer unclips and signals. The cable flies back up to the helicopter. The swimmer then makes a series of strong kicks and comes around behind Gabe, bear-hugging him around his chest.

"I'm here. You're going to be okay." The rescue swimmer's voice resonates in Gabe's ear. "Do you trust me?"

"God, yes. *Thank you.*" Gabe's voice erupts and breaks in a rush of emotion and gratitude.

A Sikorsky MH-60 Jayhawk and rescue team
at Coast Guard Air Station Kodiak

✦ ✦ ✦

The United States Coast Guard began as a small fleet of boats owned and operated by the Treasury Department in the 1790s. Secretary of the Treasury Alexander Hamilton secured funds from Congress to build ten ships to enforce the young country's trade tariffs and prevent smuggling. These ships, called "revenue cutters" or simply "cutters," were small and fast, designed to intercept and inspect arriving vessels. Our only naval force after the close of the Revolutionary War, the fleet slowly took on additional duties like rescuing ships in distress, countering piracy, and delivering mail.

More than a century later, President Woodrow Wilson signed the Coast Guard Act of 1915, creating the modern Coast Guard by merging this Revenue Cutter Service and the US Life-Saving Service, an agency tasked with preserving the lives of mariners and voyagers imperiled by shipwrecks along the eastern coast of the United States. The newly formed Coast Guard was given broad responsibilities to protect American coastal cities and waters from hostile attacks, enforce tariffs, and perform maritime search-and-rescue missions—and it still does those things today. Geographically, it's tasked with protecting the Atlantic, Pacific, and Gulf coasts, and the Great Lakes.

In 1925, the Coast Guard established Coast Guard Aviation Station Ten Pound Island in Gloucester, Massachusetts. That station acquired a squadron of seaplanes, enabling them to patrol the coast from the air and fight illegal rum-running during Prohibition. These aircraft also allowed the Coast Guard to, for the first time, render air rescue and medevac services to imperiled sailors and seagoing passengers. In the 1930s and '40s, the Coast Guard formalized an air-sea rescue service and began considering the use of helicopters.

William Kossler, a Coast Guard commander, observed a 1940 public demonstration of the Vought-Sikorsky VS-300 helicopter—the first viable American-made helicopter. Igor Sikorsky, a prolific Russian-American aviation pioneer, designed the VS-300. He also piloted the craft that day. Kossler immediately appreciated the advantages helicopters offered for maritime search and rescue, and the service branch has used them ever since.

The Coast Guard made the first helicopter rescue using a hoist and cable on November 29, 1945. That day, the Eastern Seaboard was in the grip of a massive storm blowing even harder than in the story above, at near-hurricane force. The wind and waves caused an oil barge to break free from a tanker and run aground on Penfield Reef. That particular reef lurks about a mile off the Connecticut coast and slips beneath the surface of the Long Island Sound when the tides get high. The two men aboard the barge, Captain Joseph Pawlik and crewman Steven Penninger, fired off flares when night fell and prayed for rescue as the breakers began to tear the barge apart.

People on a nearby beach spotted their flares and contacted local police. No boats could reach the imperiled vessel, though, not without endangering themselves. Fortunately for Pawlik and Penninger, Penfield Reef was only about five miles from the Sikorsky Aero Engineering Corporation facilities in Bridgeport, Connecticut.

"The police called us and said the barge was in a hell of a shape and asked if we could do anything," remembered Jimmy Viner. "I said, 'Sure could.'"[1] Viner was Igor Sikorsky's nephew and the company's chief test pilot. When he was around, courage was never a question. The following comes directly from the Sikorsky company archives:

> When the call for help came, 36-year-old Jimmy Viner yelled for a friend, Capt. Jackson E. Beighle who was an Army Air Force representative at Sikorsky. They jumped in the first available helicopter, Jimmy at the controls, and within minutes were hovering over the crippled barge, where they saw one man come out of the cabin below and set off a red flare. They dropped a rope with a weight and a message. They wanted to know how bad it was down there. In a few minutes, they pulled up

the message bag, with a return note. It was very bad. Eight tanks were leaking. The cabin was full of water. The two men were afraid the barge would break up.[2]

Viner realized that landing was impossible because of water washing over the deck, so the two men in the helicopter hatched a plan. They flew back to the Sikorsky plant and jumped into an R-5, a helicopter equipped with a hydraulic hoist. No one had ever used a hoist for this purpose, but the two men were undeterred.

"You developed faith in the machine," Viner later declared. "If you don't have that attitude, you should get out of the business." He also mentioned something else that affected his bravery that day: "God was good to me."[3] So they went.

Within minutes, the Sikorsky R-5 was hovering over the barge:

> Captain Beighle operated the rescue hoist, lowering it to the barge where Seaman Penninger looped the leather harness under his arms. Beighle raised the harness with Penninger to the cabin but could not pull him inside. Penninger hung on to Beighle while Viner flew the helicopter to the beach.
>
> After lowering Penninger to the beach, Viner took the R-5 back to the barge to pick up Captain Pawlik. When Beighle attempted to raise the hoist it jammed, leaving Pawlik suspended 30 feet (9 meters) below the helicopter. Viner again returned to the shore and carefully lowered Pawlik to the sand.[4]

A Sikorsky R-5 at Hamilton Army Airfield in
Novato, in Marin County, California

With that heroic exploit, the Coast Guard entered a new age of maritime search and rescue. Today, the service branch owns and operates forty-two Sikorsky Jayhawks and ninety-eight Eurocopter Dolphins, all of which are spread among twenty-four Coast Guard Air Stations across the United States. The dedicated men and women who operate these aircraft go out there every day to save and protect people who need help.

"We do this job because every once in a while someone is out there without hope, desperately praying for their life, and we get to be the answer," said Mario Vittone, retired chief warrant officer and rescue swimmer for Coast Guard Air Station Elizabeth City.[5]

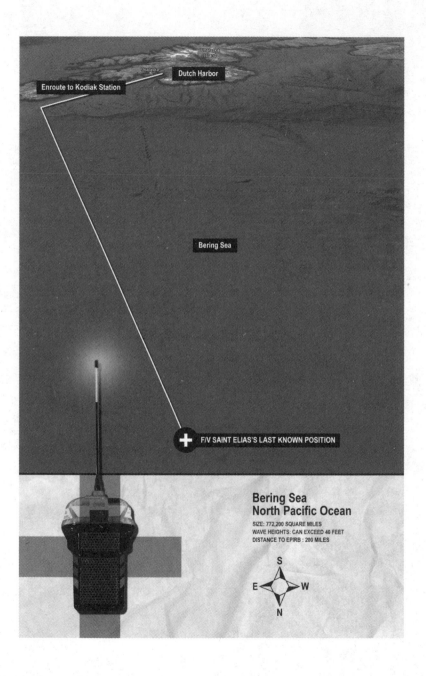

Unalaska Island

Dutch Harbor

Unalaska

Enroute to Kodiak Station

Bering Sea

✚ F/V SAINT ELIAS'S LAST KNOWN POSITION

**Bering Sea
North Pacific Ocean**

SIZE: 772,200 SQUARE MILES
WAVE HEIGHTS: CAN EXCEED 40 FEET
DISTANCE TO EPIRB : 200 MILES

BELiEF:

I DON'T NEED HELP.

Do you ever think, *I've got this. I can deal with any problem that comes. I don't need anything from anyone. Asking for help is for the weak. The only person I can rely on, anyway, is me. People just aren't trustworthy. They don't come through. They take advantage. To heck with them. It's so much better just to work harder and go it alone. To be successful on my own. To be stoic. To be a man.*

This kind of thinking is rooted neither in truth nor in the goodness of God. *Think again.*

Darkness is all around in our world. As long as we're in it, and until Jesus returns, we're going to be in continual need of rescue. It's just our reality, because this earthly landscape isn't static. The shadows are ever changing. Just when we solve one problem, another arises. After we manage to survive one crisis, another emerges. It seems to have no end, this present darkness.

But the cavalry is coming. The night may be long. The seas may be rough. We may be hurting and confused and feel like we are all alone. It might seem like all hope is lost. But it's not; rescue is at hand. *Brother, you are found. Everything's going to be okay, somehow.*

Jesus is here to deliver us out of crisis and into safety. "And after you have suffered a little while, the God of all grace, who has called you to his eternal glory in Christ, will himself restore, confirm, strengthen, and establish you" (1 Pet. 5:10). Equipped with grace unending, wielding all the incredible power of heaven, he is here to free us, heal us, and restore us—as many times as we need it. He's built a family. An army. And it's here for you. And for me. All the time.

So what's the problem?

For a few men, the problem is one of circumstances. Some men out there are facing severe illnesses. Some are incarcerated. Some have extreme professions that keep them completely isolated for long periods. For those few, authentic Christian community might be unavailable in this season. But for the rest of us—*very nearly all of us*—the reason we're not in authentic community isn't circumstances. It isn't our friends or our churches or our neighborhoods or our work. And it isn't God.

I used to think it was a combination of those factors. It was just easier to focus on other people rather than examine my own choices. After many conversations with lots of men, I've learned that most of us are in the same boat. We tend to want to focus on how the right people haven't shown up for us. How the right invitations haven't been made. Or if they have, how people in our communities haven't acted in the ways we've wanted them to act. Or maybe there's been a betrayal. Or maybe there hasn't, but it's just that our "communities" have thus far been superficial and ineffectual against real-life problems.

In most cases, though, the problem isn't any of those things. For very nearly all of us, the problem is *us*.

Wait, how's that?

Recall what the apostle Paul wrote: "By grace you have been saved through faith" (Eph. 2:8). This passage is the key to Jesus' rescue missions. It describes how our ultimate salvation works but also how *all* of his rescue missions work—even the smaller ones in which he saves us in our daily and personal circumstances.

Those few words—*by grace you have been saved through faith*—describe exactly how Jesus rescues us, even when rescue comes through the inspired words and deeds of our rescue teams. Even when it comes through the people who've been given to us to walk alongside us and provide comfort, encouragement, admonishment, prayer, mercy, material assistance, guidance, wisdom, discernment, and truth.

We are saved by grace through faith. Grace plus faith. Grace plus *trust*.

When Jesus rescued Bartimaeus from his blindness, or the sinful woman from her sin, or the man from leprosy, or the woman who had a twelve-year-old ailment that had caused constant hemorrhaging, he said the very same thing: "Thy faith hath made thee safe" (Mark 10:52; Luke 7:50; Luke 17:19; Mark 5:34).[6]

Rescue is participatory. There's a give and take. We offer our trust; Jesus provides more grace than we could ever experience in one lifetime. We offer our trust; Jesus helps us to face and/or overcome what plagues us. Our trust makes it possible for us to receive what's been available to us all along. Our trust puts us into positions that *facilitate* our own rescues.

The technical name for a Coast Guard rescue swimmer is aviation survival technician (AST). To become an AST, one must complete a grueling set of courses at the Aviation Technical Training Center (ATTC) at Air Station Elizabeth City in Elizabeth City, North Carolina. These courses cover every aspect of the job, including training on how to deal with one of the most challenging situations rescue swimmers face: a noncompliant survivor.

How many people in trouble, finding themselves injured and hypothermic, drifting alone in the open ocean, for example, would work to foil their own rescues? Well, lots of people, it turns out. Stricken by panic and shock, people in desperate straits, people who want nothing more than to be saved, can become dangerously uncooperative, sometimes even combative, toward their would-be rescuers. When adrenaline pumps, our bodies can react involuntarily. When fear grips us, we can act in ways that are quite irrational.

COAST GUARD RESCUE SWIMMERS DEPLOYED
FROM AN MH-60 JAYHAWK HELICOPTER DURING
RESCUE TRAINING IN THE ATLANTIC OCEAN

Jerry Hoover, a legend who retired with more deployments than any other Coast Guard rescue swimmer in the history of the program, described one such situation: "Panic gripped the man and he wrapped his arms around my head in a bear hug, then climbed straight up, as if standing on my head would keep him out of the water."[7] This kind of irrational fear reaction inhibits a rescue. It makes victims unrescuable.

Trainees at ATTC, therefore, learn all manner of escapes and releases. They master methods of breaking the holds of panicking victims. Hoover went on to describe how he dealt with his noncompliant survivor:

> We went deeper. My training kicked in auto-
> matically, and I used three powerful downward
> strokes. With my survivor clinging to my neck,
> I executed a front head hold release, spun him
> around, and placed him in a cross-check control
> hold, then kicked for the surface. Once we were

again breathing air, I cinched down on his chest
and finned away from the raft.[8]

When it comes to the ordinary and inevitable struggles and
hardships of life, modern men have been trained to make ourselves
unrescuable too. We're taught by culture to value independence and
self-sufficiency over all else. To distrust intimacy and community.
We've become, therefore, like noncompliant survivors. Even when it's
clear that we need help, we foil our own rescues by resisting when
people try to get close, when they try to reach out and help us in our
pain and fear.

It wasn't always so. It wasn't for me, at least. In my younger years, I
had a pack of friends in the Northern California neighborhood where
I grew up. These friendships deepened and grew through grade school,
middle school, and into high school. My priorities back then were
social status and sports, girls and grades. Okay, maybe not grades. But
among the rest, my male friendships ranked high. These guys and I
shared our fears and failures and fights. We talked about successes and
broken hearts, hopes and dreams too.

After high school, though, my priorities began to shift more
strongly toward academics. Most of my friendships in college existed
within that context. On a day-in, day-out basis, my friends became the
people in my study groups and those who were willing to grind to get
decent grades. I maintained many of my childhood friendships during
those years, but the time I devoted to them started to wane.

By my midtwenties, I'd gotten married, graduated from law school,
and put my focus squarely on building a career and a bank account.
I got "serious" and responsible, and deep-hearted friendships dropped
almost entirely off my list of top priorities. Then my wife, Jennifer, and
I had kids. And with such busy lives, how could I even think about
taking time for things that weren't focused on meeting my career goals

and my immediate family's needs? On purchasing a home and buying things to put in it?

I've been in men's ministry long enough to know that many men today can relate. But what that means is that, for most of us, our friendships are superficial, often revolving around work. Our church friendships are typically shallow too. If we're even in them, our men's groups usually have low commitments—easy ways in, easy ways out.

As the stakes have gotten higher, real friends have gotten fewer. The worries of youth and young adulthood seem tiny compared to what we're facing now. As we get older, wrote that tireless advocate for men Patrick Morley, "needs emerge that can only be met by other men—men who walk in the same shoes—men who share the same problems, men with similar life experiences—other Christian men."[9] But we lack friends like that. As life has gotten harder, right when we need authentic male fellowship, we find ourselves mostly alone.

We have nowhere to turn but to ourselves—and to the darkness.

The deck is stacked against us. Remember, this world and its culture "lies in the power of the evil one" (1 John 5:19). Jesus rules us—you and me—his followers, and he'll rule the world to come. But for now, right now, Satan holds sway over the earth. And this culture of ours almost seems like it's purpose-built to inhibit genuine masculine friendships—and it can shape us more than we care to admit. It can shape our perspectives, expectations, priorities, desires, and habits. It can, and often does, shape our ideals and images of what manhood should look like.

> "Satan watcheth for those vessels that sail
> without a convoy."[10] —George Swinnock

We are a generation of Zoom calls and electric cars, iPhones and Airbus A320s. The ages of square-rigged ships and beaver traps, railroads and robber barons have long passed. But we still pass down and perpetuate the daring and headstrong *go-it-alone* attitude that enabled men and women and families to leave their homes and cross wide and dangerous seas. We continue to instill the self-reliant and self-confident *I-don't-need-help* bearing that allowed men and women and families to push frontiers, venture into wildernesses, and survive. And we still indoctrinate our youth with the materialistic and consumeristic *anything-is-possible* ideals that have fueled the greatest economy in the world for more than a hundred years.

Strident individualism. Stubborn self-sufficiency. Single-minded ambition. These values and ideals, which were crucial in days long past, remain our values and ideals today. They run so deep it's as if they exist in our DNA. Sometimes that's a good thing. And sometimes it isn't.

The courageous, confident, self-starting, self-made, financially successful man has become the American masculine ideal. This man is strong. Always up to the task. "I've got this," he says in every situation. He doesn't need help. He's never in doubt. He's never in debt. His success is his alone. And he's who we all want and strive to be. (I sure did.)

The American masculine man doesn't need rescue. He *is* the rescuer. And what could be wrong with that?

Well, what happens when this man encounters a foe that's simply larger and more powerful than he is?

Unlike commercial airline pilots, Coast Guard rescue pilots don't make flight plans to avoid severe weather systems. They take their aircraft and aircrews right to the places on their maps where people need rescue, even if that means battling extreme rainstorms, windstorms, snowstorms, or darkness.

"People are out there in distress; it's dark, stormy … they're more than likely praying to Jesus to save them, and who comes overhead—their guardian angel in an orange helicopter," said Ken Kiest, retired chief petty officer and rescue swimmer for Coast Guard Air Station Elizabeth City.[11]

These elite rescue teams undertake thousands of missions a year. Not all are harrowing, but many of them are. And the teams undertake such missions out of a sense of duty. And they undertake them *together*. They would never think of going out alone. In this dangerous business, they know exactly how much they depend on their fellow team members.

"We succeed as a team, we fail as a team. There's no one person that can take accountability for the whole flight evolution. We're a team," said Ashlee Leppert, petty officer 2nd class and flight mechanic for Coast Guard Air Station New Orleans.[12]

Each of us is guaranteed to encounter as much fear and pain, failure and loneliness and self-doubt as any other human being. But under no circumstances can a man who aspires to the American masculine ideal ever cop to that fact. And he can never, ever ask for help. Instead, he must adopt what the sage and spiritual psychiatrist Scott Peck termed "pretended invulnerability."[13] He must act like he's got life licked.

So what options are left to such a man when he comes face to face with a problem that's too big for him to handle? Well, when his grit and gumption run out, he can turn to the material resources he commands. That approach *is* allowed. It's very much encouraged by our culture—this culture that measures a man by how little he seems to struggle and how much stuff he owns.

He's allowed to turn to professional achievement and physical acquisition. He can turn to work and titles. He can turn to what's under his control: bank and brokerage accounts, houses, cars, accoutrements of hobbies. He can turn to distractions and addictions to lessen the grief, calm the anxieties, and assuage the insecurities. To protect against the darkness, he can buy firewalls and firearms, dumbbells and dead bolts, whiskey and Wheat Thins.

What the American masculine man must *never* do, though, is turn to other people. That would require openness and vulnerability, and those are antithetical to the American masculine ideal. He mustn't stand in solidarity and victory with God and his brothers.

Even though God calls men to muster, the American masculine ideal keeps us from joining up. To do that would reveal weakness. It would mean we've failed.

This crazy problem isn't limited to American men, of course—or even to men of our generation. The so-called "mysterious visitor," a character in *The Brothers Karamazov*, saw the same thing in Russian men of the nineteenth century:

> All mankind in our age have split up into units, they all keep apart, each in his own groove; each one holds aloof, hides himself and hides what he has, from the rest, and he ends by being repelled by others and repelling them. He heaps up riches by himself and thinks, "How strong I am now and how secure," and in his madness he does not understand that the more he heaps up, the more he sinks into self-destructive impotence. For he is accustomed to rely upon himself alone and to cut himself off from the whole; he has trained himself not to believe in the help of others, in men and in humanity, and only trembles for fear he should lose his money and the privileges that he has won for himself. Everywhere in these days men have, in their mockery, ceased to understand that the true security is to be found in social solidarity rather than in isolated individual effort.[14]

We are made and meant to work, of course. We are made to create and build and earn a living. We are meant to accomplish meaningful things in this world, including providing for our family's welfare. "And God said to them, 'Be fruitful and multiply and fill the earth and subdue it, and have dominion over the fish of the sea and over the birds of the heavens and over every living thing that moves on the earth'" (Gen. 1:28).

It's not the work—nor the accomplishments, nor the money, nor the things we buy with that money—that is destructive. What is destructive is how we regard those things. What is dangerous is how we turn to those things. What we do with them. *What we ask from them.* And we ask everything. We ask them to bring us joy and peace, significance and security. We ask them to rescue us.

And they can't.

It's difficult for any man to imagine the benefit of having his own flesh-and-blood rescue team. It's hard to quantify the upside. We struggle to get our heads around how living in authentic Christian community could possibly be a hundred times better than anything we've ever experienced. It's not easy to visualize how Jesus' promise might ever become real in our own lives. Lieutenant Cummings knew it, but for those of us who are yet to experience it, it's hard to envision.

But we can certainly predict the downside. Fear grips our hearts when we think about getting real, getting vulnerable, talking about struggles and fears. Our minds fill with frightening questions like, What will our families and friends think of us if we admit we need help and ask for it? What will people think if we stop trying to live up to the American masculine ideal? We conjure images of being pitied, rejected perhaps, of losing status.

It's not worth it, our culture is quick to say. *It's imprudent.* Instead of encouraging us to turn to God and our brothers in our unease and distress, instead of encouraging us to take the way of Jesus, our culture encourages us to double down on self-rescue and physical-world-focused problem solving.

"For everyone strives to keep his individuality as apart as possible," said Dostoyevsky's mysterious visitor, "wishes to secure the greatest possible fullness of life for himself; but meantime all his efforts result not in attaining fullness of life but self-destruction."[15]

To deal with the fear and pain—the expected and very natural results of living in a world laboring under a layer of darkness—we work harder, we numb and distract more. We isolate and protect so that no one can see the real person behind the LinkedIn profile. We never allow ourselves to risk and find out and experience the upside of living in God's family, of being full members of one of his rescue teams: finding true peace, real security, actual freedom, and joy beyond our imagining.

The biggest problem with the American masculine ideal is that it's incomplete. Frontiers and fortunes aren't everything. There are other stories in our shared history—*perhaps greater stories*—that can and should animate our ideals too. It wasn't individualism or self-sufficiency that turned some of our most fraught national moments into our most proud. It was devotedness and brotherly love. It was *unity*.

United we broke free from British rule in the American War of Independence. The people of the thirteen original colonies rallied together and pulled off something the British didn't expect. Believing, as English subjects then, that it was unfair and unjust to be subjected to taxes imposed by a parliament in which we had no elected representatives, we declared our independence—and that meant war. So a bunch of poorly trained militias stood on battlefields facing an organized British Army with a seasoned officer corps. And our ragtag force compelled the British to surrender.

Commander-in-Chief George Washington called the American victory "little short of a standing miracle."[16] And he attributed the miracle to unity:

For who has before seen a disciplined Army form'd at once from such raw materials? Who, that was not a witness, could imagine that the most violent local prejudices would cease so soon, and that Men who came from the different parts of the Continent, strongly disposed, by the habits of education, to despise and quarrel with each other, would instantly become but one patriotic band of Brothers?[17]

There were dissenters, for sure. Some colonists remained loyal to monarchical rule, but far fewer than the British had expected. Leaders of the Patriots—those who supported the revolution—were able to stir the hearts of average colonists toward the cause of independence. Thomas Paine's pamphlet *Common Sense* played a crucial role in convincing colonists to come together and take up arms against England. "'Tis not in numbers," he wrote, "but in unity that our great strength lies."[18]

Great Britain was then the world's dominant industrial and maritime power. Against such a foe, no single colonial man or woman would have been foolish enough to think he or she could, all by him- or herself, force national separation from Great Britain. The idea would have been laughable.

"By uniting we stand, by dividing we fall," wrote founding father John Dickinson. Our enemy was too big to defeat on our own, so we joined forces. Under common threat, we dropped everything and rallied together. Recognizing our shared vulnerability and mutual dependency, we sacrificed and bled for one another.

And then 160 years later, *united*, we defeated the Axis powers in World War II. Not perfectly, but again we rallied. Again, we sacrificed. Again, we bled together, even though our country was in the midst of bitter racial, socioeconomic, and ideological turmoil. Even though we had isolated ourselves from our international allies in the shadow of the massive and tragic loss of life in World War I. Even though we'd let military forces deteriorate. And, because again we unified, we pulled off something equally astonishing.

In 1940, we had 175,000 active servicemen and -women, making the United States the eighteenth largest military in the world—ours was smaller than Bulgaria's.[19] Things were so bad that some of our soldiers trained with broomsticks instead of rifles.[20] We were undermanned, undertrained, and underequipped.

But when the Empire of Japan dropped bombs on our men and our ships at anchor in Pearl Harbor, we declared war once again. We rose up against our attackers—and the German Reich and the Kingdom of Italy too. The threat of these great foes shook us from our indifference and division, and once again, we enlisted. Once again, we sent men into battle: pilots and infantrymen, engineers and mechanics, intelligence officers and medics. By 1942, the ranks of our military personnel swelled to nearly four million. By 1944, those ranks stood at nearly twelve million.

In the spirit of fraternity and solidarity, we also joined forces with allies abroad—with Great Britain, France, Poland, Australia, Canada, New Zealand, South Africa, the Netherlands, Belgium, Greece, Yugoslavia, the Soviet Union, and China. United, we met the Imperial Japanese Army, the German Wehrmacht, and the Italian Royal Army in battle.

"The free men of the world are marching together to Victory!" wrote General Dwight D. Eisenhower in his Order of the Day for D-Day—June 6, 1944, the day we stormed Hitler's Fortress Europe. "In all our victorious Armies in Europe we have fought as one," wrote Winston Churchill, looking back a year later and expressing gratitude for his "brothers-in-arms." "All were together heart and soul."[21]

Our men and women back home mobilized too. Americans pulled together to equip and feed those massive armies across the oceans. We banded together and sacrificed for our brave men. "Give us strength," FDR prayed as he addressed the nation during the D-Day invasion, "strength in our daily tasks, to redouble the contributions we make in the physical and the material support of our armed forces."[22] And redouble them we did. We built massive fleets of tanks, ships, trucks, and all manner of critical war matériel.

On billboards and in store windows, on walls in waiting rooms and break rooms, in post offices and on factory floors, posters appeared: "*Together* We Win." "We Can Do It!" "Give it your best!" "Pitch in and help!" "We have just begun to fight!"[23]

Against Emperor Hirohito, Adolf Hitler, Benito Mussolini, and their forces in the field, again, no man or woman was foolish enough to step forward alone, saying to the rest of us, "Relax, I've got this." Such a thing would have been utterly ridiculous. What we did was stand again arm in arm. Again recognizing our shared vulnerability and mutual dependency, we put tensions and rivalries aside and joined forces. We built the fabled Allied Expeditionary Force. We were *for each other*. We were willing to die for one another. And *that's* what defeated the Axis powers. We were victorious because we were *united*.

Our stories of unity are as grand as any tales of individualism and self-sufficiency.

It's never un-American to join with our brothers and fight great battles against fearsome forces. It's never unmanly to be part of a squad or an outfit and call in air cover or radio for ground reinforcements when we find ourselves in a tight spot or facing higher-caliber opposition. Neglecting to do so is just incredibly foolish.

Nevertheless, we do it all the time.

In our personal lives, instead of taking advantage of the overwhelming power available to each of us in our brothers, we hold tightly to our independence and try desperately to be self-reliant.

I know because I've done it. I fell for the lie. I trusted culture and tried to be strong and go it alone, turning aside anyone who got close and tried to help. I believed that accepting help, accepting reinforcements, calling the cavalry, was somehow shameful. I would be a washout, I thought, if I weren't able to overcome every threat in my life all by myself.

Going it alone might have been okay if all I was ever up against was a minor issue at work or a small disagreement at home. It might be okay if we didn't live in a world under darkness, in a world where we're *always* under significant and imminent threat. But we do live in that world. What we're up against is the greatest enemy man has ever faced—more dangerous than any human leader, even the most evil; more fearsome than any human army, even the most savage.

The apostle John used images of giant, hideous monsters to try to convey the severity of the threat against us: "Behold, a great red dragon, with seven heads and ten horns, and on his heads seven diadems" (Rev. 12:3). "And I saw a beast rising out of the sea, with ten horns and seven heads, with ten diadems on its horns and blasphemous names on its heads. And the beast that I saw was like a leopard; its feet were like a bear's, and its mouth was like a lion's mouth" (Rev. 13:1–2).

We cannot see it, but we're up against the full menace of the "forces of evil in the heavenly places" (Eph. 6:12). We're up against the evil behind all evil.

To hold too tightly to the ideals of independence and self-reliance when facing an enemy of the magnitude of Satan and his spiritual forces makes as much sense as one of us trying to lay siege to Yorktown alone. Or one of us trying to storm the Normandy beaches all by ourselves.

> "An Army is a team. It lives, sleeps, eats, and fights as a team. This individual heroic stuff is pure horse $#!+." —General George Patton

In this fight, we need our brothers—and they need us. Against this enemy, we need to be unified. We must fight as a team. None of us is skilled enough or well-enough equipped to go it alone. In this world, in this culture, in our everyday moments, we need people next to us, walking with us, covering our six. People who are truly *for us*. People who will see it through to the very end. Only when we rally together with our rescue teams—with God and our brothers—can we overcome the darkness of this world.

David Kinnaman, president of Barna Group, a leading faith-based research firm, has directed interviews with more than two million individuals and overseen thousands of US and global research studies. Relying on the cold, hard data from one of those studies, he settled on this as fact: "Whether it's in their family, career, friendships or mental and spiritual health, men need each other—and the Church."[24]

And this is, of course, what Scripture teaches. Paul explained that, when we started following Jesus, "we all said good-bye to our partial and piecemeal lives" (1 Cor. 12:12–13).[25] Why? Because we can endure anything when we endure it together. We can overcome anything when we band together. Just like Lieutenant Cummings endured that vicious war and overcame the minutes and hours and days in those vile Japanese prison ships, we too can face anything when we stand united. With God and our brothers, we cannot fail. Our ultimate victory has already been secured; we simply must join it.

Unity. Devotedness. Brotherly love. These aren't just the most American of ideals. They are the most Christian of ideals too.

Iconic intellect Dallas Willard called us to arms: "This is an age for spiritual heroes—a time for men and women to be heroic in their faith and in spiritual character and power."[26]

This is zero hour, my brother. We're in an epic, knock-down, drag-out fight with a terrible foe. It's a battle for life and death. The battle of our lifetimes. *The battle for all time.*

And Jesus has shown us what to do. He's given us the secret to gaining strength, to thriving in dire circumstances. He's given us the formula for accessing real power, for becoming actually strong. For becoming robust men, full of joy and peace. And it isn't something any of us can accomplish directly, like with a self-help book or a wellness retreat or a TED Talk. It's achieved as a by-product of living the way he did. It's the by-product of living how Jesus calls us to live: *in community*. It's a by-product of loving the people we've been given just as much as we love ourselves.

The apostle Paul wrote, "I know how to be brought low, and I know how to abound. In any and every circumstance, I have learned the secret of facing plenty and hunger, abundance and need. I can do all things through him who strengthens me" (Phil. 4:12–13).

That was a man who truly was ready for anything. He took everything this dark world could throw at him:

> Five times I received at the hands of the Jews the forty lashes less one. Three times I was beaten with rods. Once I was stoned. Three times I was shipwrecked; a night and a day I was adrift at sea; on frequent journeys, in danger from rivers, danger from robbers, danger from my own people, danger from Gentiles, danger in the city, danger in the wilderness, danger at sea, danger from false brothers; in toil and hardship, through many a sleepless night, in hunger and thirst, often without food, in cold and exposure. (2 Cor. 11:24–27)

And *his* secret formula? It was the very same as Lieutenant Cummings's. It was doing what Jesus told us to do: living in the two greatest commandments. Loving God and loving other people also just happens to be the precise formula for living in authentic Christian community. That's why Paul devoted his life to teaching people how—and why Cummings did too in his own way two thousand years later.

This, my brother, is true masculinity. This is how we become the men we're meant to be—the fathers, husbands, friends, and leaders this world needs us to be. We become strong, not by merely acting like it, but without even thinking about it. We become tough by admitting our fears and struggles, by bringing them into the open with our close friends. We become rugged and hearty when we allow our brothers to look out for us, to help us when we need help, to help us recover when we fail, to help us get smarter, more mature, and more free. More joyful and peaceful too.

And all of this builds us into operative rescuers ourselves, fully capable of providing aid and assistance to our brothers (and our loved ones)—helping them to discover and accomplish these very same things.

False masculinity, on the other hand, distrusts and isolates and suffers alone. Instead of taking pride in being part of an elite brotherhood, it stubbornly tries to project independence and protect self-reliance. It encourages us to try to be a team unto ourselves, to block God's attempts to come for us through our brothers. And that means we never get the help we need. Rather than facing or overcoming our problems, we get stuck in them and remain there. Stuck in our bad habits, our sin, our addictions. We become impoverished, fragile, and miserable.

So, my friend, it's now time to begin turning against what culture's been telling us.

Brother, it's time to go rogue.

What does that mean for you practically? Just keep reading. That's what we jump into in the next two chapters.

— CLIP IN —
"REINFORCED"
003

D o you have a close friend?"
    Patrick Morley asked that question in his book *The Man in the Mirror.*[27] It's an essential question, one too few of us can answer in the affirmative. Sure, a few of us might fire back with a quick, *Of course I do.* But if we're honest, too many of us lack even one friend who knows everything—or almost everything—about our lives, our pasts. Most of us lack a friend whom, as Morley wrote, we "can call at 2:00 a.m."[28]

> Most men have a friendship "deficit." Their balance sheets are empty when it comes to true friends. Most men don't know how to go about developing a true friend, or how to be one. We may be surrounded by many acquaintances but lonely for someone to really talk to. We don't have someone to share our deepest dreams and fears with. We don't have anyone who is willing to just listen, to simply be a friend and listen, and not always have a quick solution.[29]

Most of us have a tough time letting people in. Letting people see us as we are—fears and pain and struggles and all. Asking for help.
    Consider these questions and capture your responses in a journal or a notes app.

003.1   What struck you about this chapter or in the story of the Coast Guard rescue? Pull out a pen or pencil or your phone and describe whatever stood out to you personally.

003.2   What do you think about these two sets of ideals: independence/self-sufficiency versus unity/brotherhood? With which set do you most closely identify? Write a few sentences explaining why. Describe your experience with each.

003.3   In his book *Life Together*, Dietrich Bonhoeffer wrote:

> Therefore, let him who until now has had the privilege of living a common Christian life with other Christians praise God's grace from the bottom of his heart. Let him thank God on his knees and declare: It is grace, nothing but grace, that we are allowed to live in community with Christian brethren.[30]

How do those words hit you? Write a few sentences explaining why the intensity of the language he used resonates with you or doesn't.

003.4   How important is it for you to have a close friend with whom you can share your heart? Imagine that something has the potential of getting in the way of a friendship like that—a great job opportunity, for example. How would you deal with it? Where does friendship fit among your highest priorities?

<< HONESTLY, NOT VERY HIGH - - - - - - - - IT'S VERY IMPORTANT TO ME >>
     1   2   3   4   5   6   7   8   9   10

Whatever number you've chosen, write a few sentences explaining why it would be difficult or easy or somewhere in between.

003.5   Do you have a 2:00 a.m. friend? Imagine calling a friend and being honest with him about what you're struggling with right now. Imagine how you'd start the conversation. Imagine him asking you deep, penetrating questions. Imagine not having all the answers and asking him for help or advice. How hard would that kind of talk be? Circle a number below:

<< I'LL CALL HIM RIGHT NOW - - - - - - - - - - - YEAH, I DON'T THINK SO >>

1   2   3   4   5   6   7   8   9   10

Whatever number you've chosen, write a few sentences explaining why it would be difficult or easy or somewhere in between.

And if you do have a 2:00 a.m. friend, send him a text or an email or give him a call right now and tell him how grateful you are to have a friend like him. If you don't have such a friend, spend a few more minutes considering why you don't. Write a few sentences about it. Permission to be honest is granted.

003.6   See if you can recall a time or two when you probably should have asked for help but didn't. And then consider a time or two when you *did* ask for help—and accepted it. What are your feelings about those times? How did they turn out?

Jot down your thoughts about these various incidents and how they went. Feel free to go wherever you want. There are no right or wrong answers.

Experiment with listening prayer. Find a place where you can sit comfortably for twenty to thirty minutes, a place you're unlikely to be interrupted. Ask the Holy Spirit to direct your thoughts. Pray against distraction, against fatigue, against confusion. Now, first, just remain quiet for a length of time. Whatever feels right. Just breathe and relax. Enjoy a few moments of solitude.*

---

* For a full explanation and discussion of listening prayer, please refer to chapter 3 in the first book in the WiRE Series for Men, *Invention: Break Free from the Culture Hell-Bent on Holding You Back.*

Then, when you're ready, ask God this question: *Are there any ways that I've been blocking your attempts to love and help me? Have there been times when you've wanted to come for me through another person, but I've made myself unrescuable and turned them away?*

Now, sit quietly for ten to twenty minutes. Don't feel any pressure to hear anything from God. And don't rush it. Don't try to listen with your physical ears but with your heart. See what thoughts come. Listen for an inner voice. Maybe it will come and maybe it won't.

Then, when the time is done, in one or two sentences, describe whatever words or ideas or pictures came to mind, if any.

Pray right now.

> *Jesus, my life is busy and complicated, and sometimes it's just plain hard. I'm often weary and overwhelmed. And too often, instead of turning to you, I turn to things that ultimately do more harm than good. But I want to change. I'm asking you, now, for your help. I am calling out for rescue.*
>
> *Help me align my priorities with yours. It's hard even saying those words. So I'll repeat them: Help me align my priorities with yours. Help me to want your rescue, not avoid it. Help me to welcome your rescue, not foil it. Help me to want to grow and get healthy by allowing you in. Help me to get stronger by lowering my defenses.*
>
> *I'm going to let you in. Help me let you in.*
> *Amen.*

GOOD GRACE

People
Come together
Strange as neighbors
Our blood is one

// Joel Houston, songwriter

DSVS AND ROVS AND TRUST

Two men are trapped 659 feet down in dark, nearly freezing water. They've been stuck fast for the last three days. Inside their capsule, they've run out of water and food and are quickly running out of oxygen—and hope. The only thing they have in abundance is carbon dioxide.

But they have too much of that. Each breath uses up a bit more O_2 and poisons the air with a bit more CO_2.

In situations like this, it's all about time. And these men don't have much left.

Douglas Pritchard and Juan Thomas are maritime archaeologists. They colead a joint venture between the Canadian government and two esteemed research institutes: the Quebec-based Interdisciplinary Centre for Hydrography and the Massachusetts-based New Bedford Institution of Oceanographic Research. Dr. Pritchard works for the Canada Parks Underwater Archaeology Team. Dr. Thomas works for New Bedford, a center renowned for its exploration of the deepest parts of the world's oceans.

But these men aren't in any ocean right now. They're down in the murky deep of the St. Lawrence River. They were exploring the wreck of the HMCS *Charlottetown*, a Canadian warship that was sunk there by two Nazi torpedoes nearly eighty years ago.

Back then, the St. Lawrence was a critical route connecting Canadian cities to the Allied troops fighting on World War II's Western Front, supplying them with the desperately needed necessities for making war—things like armaments, ammunition, vehicles, gasoline, fuel oil, and food. The Battle of the St. Lawrence pitted North American convoys against submarines sent across the Atlantic by Hitler to hunt for easy prey and staunch the great flow of soldiers and supplies.

From May 1942 to November 1944, German U-boats sank twenty-three merchant ships and warships in this conflict. Two U-boats alone, U-517 and U-165, working together over three weeks in August and September of 1942, managed to sink twelve vessels, including the *Charlottetown*.

Drs. Pritchard and Thomas were seeking to rediscover and retrace the rich history of this battle. Their goals were to locate and explore each of these wrecks, bring to life the stories of these convoys, and memorialize the men lost.

The *Charlottetown* was a 208-foot corvette-style warship designed to be an anti-submarine convoy escort. On September 11, 1942, captained by Lieutenant Commander John Bonner, the vessel had just escorted convoy SQ-35 safely into the port at Rimouski and was headed to its base at Gaspé. But about halfway back, cruising downriver alongside the HMCS *Clayoquot*, a minesweeper, it took two torpedoes aft from a skulking U-517, and it went down fast.

Sixty-four souls were aboard. The captain and eight crew members perished, mostly from the explosions. The remaining fifty-six crew members were plucked from the water by the *Clayoquot* just as the *Charlottetown* settled onto the river bottom.

Then, three days ago, at eight o'clock in the morning, Drs. Pritchard and Thomas climbed into their deep-water research submarine, the *Emmett*, named for the craft's inventor, Robert Emmett. The submersible is owned by the United States Office of Naval Research but operated by the New Bedford Institution. Once launched, it took the men less than ten minutes to dive and reach that same pitch-black riverbed. The mission was scheduled to last six hours.

The *Emmett*, a deep-submergence vehicle (DSV), is designed to access waters much deeper than 600 feet. The craft's test depth rating is a whopping 20,000 feet, which means it can access 98 percent of the world's ocean floors. To withstand those crushing pressures, the crew compartment is constructed as a sphere with two-inch-thick titanium walls. It also has a small hatch, five small viewports, and loads of electronic and computing gear. The men and women who operate the *Emmett* call their compartment "the Ball."

Drs. Pritchard and Thomas spent that first day taking notes and pictures from all available angles. Then, at 2:00 p.m., with the *Emmett*'s battery all but drained, they peered one last time into one of the gaping and unnatural holes blown in the *Charlottetown*'s hull.

And that's when it happened.

Both men winced at the soft but discordant sound of metal bumping metal. Dr. Thomas, the pilot for their trip, cursed and immediately engaged the craft's reverse thrusters. As the submarine began to pull back, a whole mess of eighty-year-old cables and debris crashed over the submersible. The sudden, awful clanging and scraping contrasted wildly with the sounds they'd been listening to all day: the soft hum of the CO_2 scrubbers (which remove dangerous carbon dioxide from the craft's atmosphere) and the quiet whirr of the *Emmett*'s small propellers.

Dr. Thomas hit reverse hard and backed away from the wreck— except he couldn't. The vessel had become ensnared in the tangle of rusted cables.

"Hey, Juan, buddy," Dr. Pritchard said, "I think we might be in a bit of trouble."

For two hours, the men attempted to secure their own release using the vessel's seven directional thrusters, moving this way and that. They also engaged the *Emmett*'s two hydraulic robotic arms to try to free themselves. The only success they had, though, was in becoming even more entangled in the web of corroded steel.

It wasn't the first time a deep-water submergence vehicle had gotten itself stuck. And the *Emmett* was actually designed to handle emergencies like this. Its outer body—the shell that surrounds the Ball and houses the propulsion systems, batteries, ballast tanks, hydraulics, and propellers—can break open and allow the titanium personnel sphere to escape and rise by itself to the surface. The problem for the trapped researchers, though, is that those blasted cables wouldn't allow the outer body to separate.

When the men finally gave up their struggle, they'd been underwater for a total of eight hours, communicating the entire time with the R/V *Naushon* via the *Emmett*'s acoustic transmission system. The *Naushon* is a 142-foot, state-of-the-art oceanographic research ship, and it's the surface vessel supporting this mission. So, out of options, Drs. Pritchard and Thomas and the captain of the *Naushon* had no choice but to send out that rarest and most critical of distress signals: SUBSUNK.

The Canadian Marine Communications and Traffic Services (MCTS) monitor VHF radio frequencies 24 hours a day, 365 days a year, listening for maritime distress signals. When they receive one, the hardworking people manning the radios relay those signals to the appropriate search-and-rescue services. In this case, the MCTS sent the *Emmett*'s mayday to Coast Guard Base Quebec, which houses the Maritime Rescue Sub-Centre.

Because of the submerged nature of the mission, the Sub-Centre tossed the mayday call across the Atlantic to a small, nondescript office in northwest London. The International Submarine Escape and Rescue Liaison Office (ISMERLO) is an intergovernmental humanitarian organization that coordinates rapid responses to submarine accidents. These folks are on constant standby and will do just about anything to save the lives of their brave undersea sailor brethren.

Wasting no time, ISMERLO immediately published the distress signal on its private website. The notice included GPS coordinates, the stricken vessel's status, and the number of people aboard. And the site lit up. Rescue teams from ISMERLO member nations began responding and offering rescue systems/approaches and times to first rescue (TTFR). A TTFR is a realistic estimated timeline for a particular team to arrive on scene and commence rescue operations. It is crucial because it allows nations requesting assistance to choose the best from among all the available options—and when one is dealing with a distressed sub, best usually equals fastest.

The Americans responded first. Their TTFR didn't look good, though, because their submersible was already in action in Hawaii. The Japanese were next. Then the Brits. The UK Submarine Rescue Team is generally considered the world's best. Based outside of Glasgow, Scotland, the mission of this small, elite outfit is to be able to reach any stricken sub anywhere in the world in under seventy-two hours from SUBSUNK.

John Hatfield heads the UK Sub Rescue's Scorpio team. Like the *Emmett*, the *Scorpio* is a deep-water submersible. Unlike the *Emmett*, though, the *Scorpio* is an unmanned, remotely operated vehicle (ROV). Lieutenant Commander Hatfield is the *Scorpio*'s primary pilot, and he responded to the *Emmett*'s mayday because his machine is equipped with cutters that can make quick work of almost any steel cable.

When the Canadian Coast Guard saw Hatfield's TTFR, they gave him the green light.

Hatfield's team is on constant twelve-hour standby, so he had that long to get his team and equipment into a C-17 Globemaster and get that massive transport plane into the air. Once loaded and en route, the flight to Quebec would take six and a half hours. Then the drive to Cap-Chat, a small town with a small harbor where Hatfield could meet the *Naushon* and load the *Scorpio* onto the ship, would take roughly another five.

Assuming standard loading and unloading times for airplanes and trucks and boats—plus the time it would take to move the *Naushon* into the right spot on the river, launch the *Scorpio*, and position it to do the necessary cutting—Hatfield's estimate had him getting the *Scorpio* into the water and down to the stricken submarine about six hours under the UK Submarine Rescue Team's goal of seventy-two hours.

The only problem was that the *Emmett* had seventy-two hours of life support when it initially launched—nine bottles of aviator-grade oxygen—and Drs. Pritchard and Thomas used up eight of those before they sent out their distress signal. So the math didn't actually look that great, and that clock just kept ticking. If he wasn't able to shave some time off that TTFR, Hatfield knew things were going to get very dicey very quickly.

A British Scorpio ROV retrieved during the rescue of the Russian Priz class submersible AS-28 trapped on the seafloor off the Kamchatka Peninsula in 2005

Inside the cramped metal bubble, it's cold, damp, pitch dark, and quiet. Batteries dead, the men haven't been able to communicate with the surface for nearly forty-eight hours.

During this time of year, water temperatures in the St. Lawrence hover around 35 degrees Fahrenheit, and the submersible isn't heated. Fortunately, it's standard operating procedure for crews to bring warm clothing along on their dives. Around noon on their first day, the men started adding layers. Wool socks. Wool beanies. Thick sweatpants. Dr. Pritchard donned an Irish fisherman's sweater, Dr. Thomas a Cornell hoodie.

Drs. Pritchard and Thomas also brought water bottles and a thermos full of coffee. Not knowing what lay ahead, though, both men drank the contents of their water bottles on the first day. *Emmett* explorers usually avoid the coffee because the only way for them to relieve themselves is into a plastic jug, which they have dubbed the "endurance range extender."

On this trip, however, the men have carefully rationed that precious liquid over the past fifty or so hours. But it's nowhere near enough fluid, and both men have become severely dehydrated. The men also brought food but ate most of it for lunch on day one: ham and cheese sandwiches, a couple of apples, two candy bars. They did save two peanut butter and jelly sandwiches for the trip back to the surface, however. So the men have rationed these as well. But they ate the last small bites more than twelve hours ago.

The excess CO_2, plus their lack of water and food, mean the men are sleeping for long periods, and when they're awake, their minds are foggy. Even simple tasks are requiring way more time and mental energy than usual.

At this point, the only light available to the men is from a single digital wristwatch, which they use to track how many hours they've been down in these abysmal depths. But the simple addition and subtraction necessary to calculate that time is getting harder and harder to do.

These men are fading fast.

Then, at 7:23 a.m., Dr. Thomas comes out of a shallow sleep, awakened by a faint sound: the whirr of a submersible's thruster. He hasn't heard that sound in more than two days. He considers the genuine possibility that he might be hallucinating. He strains to listen between Dr. Pritchard's ragged breaths. When he doesn't hear it again, he drifts off back to sleep. He soon wakes again, though, this time to the shrill and unmistakable sound of a rotating blade cutting through steel.

"Oh, thank God. Doug. Doug! Wake up, buddy. Wake up. I think they've found us!"

Overcome with joy and relief, Dr. Thomas shakes Dr. Pritchard awake.

"I think we're going to be okay, Doug. I think they're going to get us the heck out of here."

✚ ✚ ✚

People have been experimenting with submarines since the sixteenth century. It wasn't until the turn of the twentieth, though, that designers adequately addressed the pesky issues that had plagued prior generations of underwater pioneers: finding appropriate means of propulsion, submergence, and maintaining balance underwater. They were also able to deal with dangerous physiological problems like how to deal with foul air and decompression sickness.

With these developments, submarines began to be used widely: in warfare to attack enemy vessels with torpedoes and launch missiles, both conventional and nuclear; for espionage operations; and for science to explore the world's oceans.

Concurrent with these military and scientific endeavors, however, tragedies occurred. Many thousands of submariners lost their lives in the great naval battles of the two World Wars. And more were lost to accidents before, between, and after them.

Most of those disasters resulted in quick deaths for the sailors aboard the doomed subs, either from explosion (from torpedoes, depth charges, and mines) or implosion (when impaired vessels descended below their crush depths). But others didn't.

In some cases, submarines became disabled in waters shallow enough for survivors to be trapped but to hold out hope of escape. However, those trapped men faced three new horrors: asphyxia (from falling oxygen levels), CO_2 poisoning (from rising carbon dioxide levels), and hypothermia (from dropping temperatures). If that wasn't enough, many crews faced two other potential dangers: flooding and fire.

Having no viable way to save sailors entrapped in sunken submarines, the navies of the world mourned their losses and generally consigned these unfortunate souls to their gruesome fates.

All of that changed, though, when in May 1939, the USS *Squalus* sank during sea trials several miles off Portsmouth, New Hampshire. An engine induction valve failed, causing the vessel's torpedo room, engine rooms, and crew quarters to flood—drowning twenty-six men. The thirty-three remaining submariners acted quickly and prevented further flooding. But they couldn't stop the damaged sub from sinking to the seafloor. Fortunately for the men aboard, the Atlantic isn't very deep in that area, and the vessel came to a rest at a depth of 243 feet.

Because the sub was performing a test dive when disaster struck, companion and support vessels were nearby. As a result, the mayday went out quickly, and a rescue ship was soon on scene.

Rescue operations commenced under the direction of submarine rescue legend Lieutenant Commander Charles Momsen. Momsen and his team deployed what's called a McCann Rescue Chamber. The contraption is a pear-shaped steel chamber that can be lowered to a stricken vessel and attached to its escape hatch, allowing imperiled sailors to climb up and aboard. On that day, all thirty-three surviving crew members were rescued in four trips from the surface to the seafloor and back.

The *Squalus* rescue heralded a new era of submarine rescue operations. No longer would so many submariners have to perish beneath the waves. And since then, systems and procedures have improved dramatically. Today, ISMERLO is made up of rescue teams from Australia, Brazil, China, France, India, Italy, Japan, South Korea, Norway, Singapore, Spain, Sweden, Turkey, the United States, and the United Kingdom. Together they offer a wide variety of sophisticated surface and support ships, ROVs, DSVs, and recompression chambers.

The British Royal Navy even has an elite squad it calls the Submarine Parachute Assistance Group. These servicemen and -women can be activated on six hours' notice and will fly directly to the site of a SUBSUNK incident, parachute to the surface of the ocean, and provide any survivors who might have escaped a sinking sub with rafts, food, water, medical assistance, and life support.

And all of these things—personnel and equipment—are focused on a single mission: saving the lives of submariners at sea.

Grand Fonds

Le Village-du-Cap

Le Boom

Cap-Chat, Canada

St. Lawrence River

Wreck of the HMCS Charlottetown

St. Lawrence River
Cap-Chat, Canada

EST. TIME TO FIRST RESCUE: 66 HOURS
WATER TEMPERATURE: 35° F
DEPTH OF WRECK: 659 FEET

BELiEF:

I'LL FIGURE IT OUT.

Do you ever think, *Look, I'm doing fine. I know tons of people. And if I do ever decide to hang closely with some other men, I'm going to make darn sure they're* my *kind of guys. Good guys. Because I don't need anyone acting strange around me. I don't need to be around a bunch of misfits. And no matter what, I'm not going to be super open, either. That would be weird. Real men don't blather on.*

This kind of thinking is rooted neither in truth nor in the goodness of God. *Think again.*

What exactly *is* community anyway? The word has already appeared many times in these pages. Pastors give sermons on the importance of it. Tech companies create software and apps to help churches build it. YouTube offers videos about all its various aspects. Christian media outlets publish articles with titles like "5 Tips for Community" and "Why Community Is So Important." Churches even put the word right into their names.

And the Christian world isn't alone; the broader world uses the word too, but mostly to describe neighborhoods or towns. Or to describe groups of people who share common characteristics, experiences, values, or interests and are living or working or studying somewhere together.

In nearly all of these cases, the definitions are loose. And that's part of the problem.

Modern men don't lack loose-definition communities. We have neighborhood communities. Work communities. Church communities. We have communities that form around hobbies and sports and past schooling and our children's activities. We belong to lots of those.

What we tend to lack are communities that meet a narrower definition. So what is that?

Narrow-definition community (=) authentic Christian community. It is community rooted in the way of Jesus. But even more than that, it actually includes and involves the very *presence* of Jesus himself. It's a mystical thing and therefore mysterious. It's something to be experienced and enjoyed more than dissected and defined. But to encourage you, my friend, into a more profound experience of it, here's what I know about the basics.

Authentic Christian community is a creation of God, and it looks like something he'd create. It looks like *him*, actually. It looks like the Trinity: multiple persons choosing to be joined together in honesty and sacrificial love.

Community isn't an organization. It isn't a "place to which we go," wrote Rufus Jones, Quaker theologian and philosopher; it's "something we do."[1] It forms when we meet our brothers and God in truth and love and engage in prayer, study, worship, conversation, encouragement, confession, accountability, service, celebration, or any good combination of these things.

In authentic Christian communities, we speak about our lives and our pasts, not just about joys and successes, but fears and failures too. We invest ourselves and prioritize one another. We are *for* one another in meaningful ways, even in the midst of our busy and challenging lives. We meet on a frequent and regular basis. We commit to being present for one another—physically and mentally.

The difference between being part of a community with a more flexible definition and being part of an authentic Christian community is the difference between having mere friends and being blessed with *true* friends, between knowing guys and having *real* brothers.

Authentic Christian communities come in different sizes and arrangements. They can be formal, traditional, relaxed, or renegade. They can be Monday morning Bible studies at our workplaces or monastic orders in far-off mountains. They can work like typical Bible study groups; standard church men's ministries; prayer groups;

accountability groups; twelve-step programs; all-in, live-in communities; and many other formations.

Authentic Christian community is, wrote Dutch theologian and humanitarian Henri Nouwen, more than anything else, a "way of living."[2] And whenever we engage in it, sooner or later—typically *very* soon—we discover something of tremendous power and capability: Lieutenant Cummings's secret. We come upon something that's finally able to pull us out of the darkness of this world and heal us and connect us back with God. We uncover the very thing Jesus announced two millennia ago, that thing he promised would be one hundred times better than anything else this world has to offer.

Loose-definition communities form because we like one another, live close to one another, or engage in a common endeavor. Authentic Christian community comes into being because we hear a whisper in our hearts inviting us toward God, toward certain brothers, and toward honesty and love. "The basis of the Christian community," wrote Nouwen, "is not the family tie, or social or economic equality, or shared oppression or complaint, or mutual attraction, but the divine call."[3] We need narrow-definition communities because God designed us to need them. We desire them because he embeds the desire into our hearts. We gather because he summons us.

The saints agree. We don't form community by choice or by chance. Trappist monk and mystic Thomas Merton wrote that authentic Christian community "is not built by man; it is built by God."[4] And Oxford and Cambridge don C. S. Lewis wrote this:

> Christ, who said to the disciples, "Ye have not chosen me, but I have chosen you," can truly say to every group of Christian friends, "You have not chosen one another but I have chosen you for one another."[5]

And yet, when we men finally accept that we're designed for community, we nearly always try to wrest control of the process. We use stated or unstated criteria and start trying to find the "right" men. (I've done that.) We scheme and single out guys who are cool or rich or connected or well-educated or who would be good to know from a work perspective. And if we don't fall into those traps, we choose guys who are simply a lot like us.

We lean in or move away from other men based on our rankings and ratings. We think, *If I'm going to devote myself to a handful of other guys, they're going to have some strategic value to me—worldly value to my career or my social standing or my interests—or at the very least, they're going to be men who won't question or confront me or make me too uncomfortable.*

When we come across men who don't meet those criteria, we rarely ask, "Could these *still* be the right men for me? Could these be men whom *God* has brought to me? Could *this* be the makings of a rescue team?" No, we resist. Because they don't look right. They're in the wrong business or have the wrong enthusiasms. Run in the wrong social circles or live in the wrong neighborhoods. They're too awkward or too put together. Too loud or too quiet. Too outgoing or too dull. They challenge us too much—or in the wrong ways.

If we somehow find our way into groups that may have seemed okay at first but are now falling short of our ideals, we plan our escape. Rather than bear down and work through the inevitable differences and difficulties, the awkwardness and misunderstandings, the tensions and painful interactions, we abandon ship.

We want ideal groups, designed to our standards. But those kinds of "ideal" groups are not narrow-definition communities. They're actually just more loose-definition communities, and in them we rarely, if ever, find rescue. In them, we usually remain trapped by the darkness.

The process of forming and maintaining authentic Christian community is simply too complicated. Only God can grasp and navigate the totality of things, things like our backgrounds, our wounds, our annoying and strange personal habits, the relative rates at which we're willing and able to change. And of course, our fallen natures, by which

I mean our proclivities for laziness and carelessness, our tendencies toward pride and selfishness, cruelty and offense.

Creating authentic community will always remain "the intricate, patient, painful work of the Holy Spirit," wrote Eugene Peterson, Presbyterian pastor and poet.[6] Uniting us, providing each of us with *who we need* and *what we need* and all of it *when we need it* is just far beyond our finite abilities. We have too little knowledge and intellect, too little brute strength to create something as wondrous, wonderful, and otherworldly as authentic Christian community.

And when we attempt to engineer our own men's groups, ignoring God's voice, we miss the cosmic gift our loving God has for us. We create groups that kind of look like authentic community but aren't. "We end up settling for ... an occasionally convincing counterfeit of community" wrote Larry Crabb.[7] These are "religious clubs," not "resurrection communities," wrote Eugene Peterson.[8]

But we can survive with loose-definition communities for a long time and even think we're doing okay. Shallow associations and thin interactions do offer some benefits, of course. They're just a far cry from what authentic community provides. If we maintain our refusals, therefore, it might never dawn on us what we're missing—that thing Bonhoeffer called an "unspeakable gift of God."[9] We might forever miss the miracle of *real* community and the miracles that happen in such fellowships—and never even know it.

When I walked into the Cave on that otherwise dreary day more than ten winters ago, I sure didn't know what I'd been missing. Fortunately, because I surrendered and simply showed up, because I somehow dragged myself and my weary heart into that conference room that day, I soon found out. And it blew my mind.

I found God's unspeakable gift. I found the secret—the thing that's available and intended to help us survive and even thrive during these evil days.

I found my rescue team.

The massive nuclear-powered, Oscar-class submarine K-141 *Kursk* sank on August 12, 2000, in the Barents Sea. Somehow, an old and faulty torpedo exploded in one of the vessel's torpedo tubes. The ensuing inferno then caused several more torpedoes to explode, which tore an enormous hole in the boomer's hull. Most of the crew was killed in the two explosions, but twenty-three Russian sailors were able to seal themselves in an aft compartment.

Fearing international embarrassment, Russian leaders refused offers of assistance from more capable rescue teams from other nations, even though the Russian Navy had repeatedly failed in its attempts to rescue the trapped men. The Russian newspaper *Segodnya* wrote, "The admirals think everything will end in political catastrophe if a single Russian sailor is rescued from a Russian submarine with foreign help."[10]

No one knows for sure how long those twenty-three men survived. It was long enough, though, for them to write heart-wrenching letters to their loved ones. (The messages were found during salvage.) But by the time British and Norwegian rescue teams were finally allowed to reach the sub and open its hatches, the men had perished.

K-141 *KURSK* NUCLEAR SUBMARINE DOCKED AT
VIDYAYEVO NAVAL BASE IN MURMANSK OBLAST,
RUSSIA, JUST PRIOR TO ITS FATEFUL VOYAGE

ISMERLO was founded in the wake of the *Kursk* disaster. An international team of military officers and engineers came together to help the world avoid this kind of petty but deadly geopolitical maneuvering. The dedicated men and women of ISMERLO try to be open and unbiased. Humble and earnest. They maintain a high and constant level of operational readiness. On very short notice, they'll drop everything; jump into planes, trucks, and automobiles; and go anywhere in the world to provide whatever assistance they can to any nation that requests its help.

Gennaro Vitagliano, commander in the Italian Navy and head of ISMERLO, summed up the organization's philosophy:

> We are talking about saving lives at sea. We don't make any distinction between saving a life or another life. For us, it's an important brotherhood. For us, it's important to be here and be ready to save a life—whatever country this life belongs to.[11]

The Russian Federation has now become a member of ISMERLO too.

When God chooses us for one another, he takes great care. He might select people because of their loyalty and friendship, or it might be because of their love of him and their gift of wisdom. Or he might choose people who will reveal things in us and help us grow—or people whom *we* can help to grow. He might select people because they'll challenge or contradict us. Or maybe because they'll trigger impatience. Undoubtedly, he'll choose people because he knows they will shape us in beautiful ways and teach us how to love better.

He might choose people for us from similar or different places or kinds of families, from similar or different backgrounds or ethnicities, from similar or different socioeconomic or employment statuses. He might choose people from similar or different ages or stages of life, from similar or different stages or rates of spiritual growth.

This often means that the men chosen for us will look very different from the men we might choose for ourselves, because the men we would choose for ourselves—men who affirm us and make us feel good about ourselves—are never the ones likely to challenge us, sharpen us, and help us become the men we're meant to be.

In the late summer of 2010, the Cave had gotten too large for the faux stone conference room, and I began kicking around the idea of breaking off and starting a new group. That's right, the guy who could barely walk into the building a year and a half prior was now thinking about taking the show on the road.

I emailed Brenden and another friend. I shared with them my ideas, especially about the specific men I was hoping to invite into community. The guys I had in mind were about the same ages as the three of us were. Most were married with young children. All were working long hours. And all were isolated, just like we had been.

We reached out to a few of them to gauge interest. And by September, our new group was up and running. We met around the conference table in my venture capital office. So that's what we called ourselves: *the Table*.

The first few meetings were mostly just us, the three cofounders. Guys would attend and then drop off. We tried to lead like the leaders of the Cave had taught us, with vulnerability and boldness. But things stagnated—until we did something revolutionary: we turned the roster over to God.

We prayed, *Forget who we want, God. Just bring the right men, whoever they are.* We even prayed, *Keep the wrong men away.* And God surprised us. The group began to grow. A crew of committed men took shape. An authentic but unexpected rescue team formed.

We had men who were executives at tech companies. We had men who worked at law firms, venture capital firms, private equity firms, and investment banks. We had programmers, real estate agents, contractors, financial advisers, a physical therapist, a teacher, a firefighter, and an amazing man who worked for a lumber company. We had men who worked for nonprofits and in minimum wage jobs in retail stores. We had men who owned retail stores. And we had guys who were temporarily out of work.

We had men in their twenties and men in their sixties. We had men of different national descents and geographical experiences. We had men who grew up in Christian homes and in nonbelieving ones too. We had men who were newly married, men who'd been married a long time, single men, and divorced men. We had men with young children, men whose children were grown, and men without any children at all.

And we got vulnerable. Deep friendships formed. We argued. We laughed a lot. We worshipped. We shared meals. We prayed a ton. And breakthroughs happened. God moved in power—in the sin and friction, anger and annoyance, spontaneous joy and surprising solidarity. *United*, we got free of some of the things that had been plaguing our lives. It was glorious.

"Christian brotherhood," wrote Dietrich Bonhoeffer, "is not an ideal which we must realize; it is rather a reality created by God in Christ in which we may participate."[12]

If we want to try to control and manage our communities, he'll let us. If we're going to step into community only partway, he'll let us. If we want to avoid community altogether, he'll let us. And he'll let us face the consequences too.

For all his interest and involvement in forming narrow-definition communities, he only ever invites us into them. He asks. He woos. For all his power and might, he never forces anything on us, because true love is never coercive. And if we choose not to join one of his communities, he'll simply and quietly ask us again and again and again.

This is counterintuitive for modern American men, but our job is never to design or craft or control our rescue teams. Nor is it to question why or when or how God initiates them for us—or why he doesn't. Our job is simply to get on board with what he's already doing. It's to humble ourselves, surrender our need for control, and try to discern what and when and how he's been building community for us already, and then to support those efforts with all of our hearts.

When SUBSUNK blinks on the ISMERLO hub, the details are important. Accuracy is crucial. Truth is essential. If facts are conveyed incorrectly or suppressed because they might embarrass the nation whose submarine is in distress, then the organization cannot do its job. If the various member nations' sub rescue teams cannot plan and prepare for the precise situation, they'll lose precious time. And human beings can die, like they did with the *Kursk*.

Authentic community operates on honesty too. Truth—the whole truth and nothing but the truth. It's the basis of any meaningful relationship, and it's no different for rescue teams. For them to even form in the first place, and indeed for them to work properly going forward, we men must be known by our brothers. To love each other truly, not partially, we must know each other fully, not partially.

We must be willing to share the good and the bad, the best and the worst of who we are and what we've done. Being forthright with one another creates intimacy and trust. A lack of truth—withholding, denying, lying, covering up our fears and failures—clouds and confuses things and creates division. Refusals to share our stories and confess to one another just prolong separation.

In authentic community, we stand for one another, as Bonhoeffer wrote, "in Christ's stead."[13] When we hide things from our brothers, we effectively hide ourselves from the healing, rescuing power of Jesus. A lack of honesty impedes the miraculous.

To rescue us from the darkness and bring us into the light, our brothers need to know about the darkness that exists in our hearts and our lives. Hiding prevents our brothers from being moved to pray fervently, effectively, and efficiently. It limits our abilities to offer each other grace-fueled wisdom and truth. It interferes with our abilities to be kind and merciful and accepting of each other's flaws and failures, because often we don't even know they're there or we can't see them clearly. It also inhibits our abilities to keep each other accountable.

Jesus said, "My power is made perfect in weakness" (2 Cor. 12:9). When we are vulnerable with one another, we experience more of that power in our lives. "Therefore," concluded the apostle Paul, "I will boast all the more gladly of my weaknesses, so that the power of Christ may rest upon me.... For when I am weak, then I am strong" (2 Cor. 12:9–10).

Rescue teams can swing into action when members stop posturing and pretending and trying to prove themselves, stop competing and hurting one another. When our brothers can see us as we are and we can see them—our personalities, flaws, weaknesses, sins, mistakes, fears, dreams, struggles, stories—we can all focus on real needs, not facades. And then breakthroughs can happen. When we deal with each other honestly, we deal with God honestly—and that's when he can move with great power.

If honesty and vulnerability are crucial to the operation of rescue teams, and if we're built to be in close relationship with a few close compatriots, why do so few of us get honest and vulnerable? The answer is simple, and it's always the same. We don't because we're ashamed. And we're afraid. (I have been.) Shame is something *all* human beings experience. And we always have, going back to the first humans. Just as Adam and Eve were ashamed by their brokenness, so are we.

> And they heard the sound of the LORD God walking in the garden in the cool of the day, and the man and his wife hid themselves from the presence of the LORD God among the trees of the garden. But the LORD God called to the man and said to him, "Where are you?" And he said, "I heard the sound of you in the garden, and I was afraid, because I was naked, and I hid myself." (Gen. 3:8–10)

We're ashamed of our bad choices, known flaws, backgrounds, looks, and résumés. In our deepest places, what we fear is disconnection. Brené Brown, researcher and remarkable TED Talker, wrote that shame is "the fear that something we've done or failed to do, an ideal that we've not lived up to, or a goal that we've not accomplished makes us unworthy of connection."[14] We're afraid that if families and friends and acquaintances knew the whole story, they wouldn't accept or love us anymore.

This will resonate with some guys right away. They know shame; they feel it. Others may not. Often that's because the shame lies a bit deeper, for it is shame that drives our need to overachieve. It's our feelings of not being smart enough, good enough, or man enough that cause us to let our work go beyond providing for the needs of our families and to get in the way, actually, of our relationships *with* our families. It's our perceived need to prove ourselves that leaves us with no time for authentic community.

Whether we hide because we are ashamed outright or because we are too relentlessly focused on ourselves, our careers, our own advancement, and our accumulation, it's just a fact that most modern Christian men hide. Giving anyone the whole truth of our lives is exceedingly rare in this world of ours. Even with family members and closest friends, we tend to reveal only certain parts of our stories and lives.

And it's easy. Our neighbors are different from our friends at church. Our colleagues at work are different from the parents at our kids' schools. We work with some people, not others. We socialize with some, not others. We intersect at church with some, not others. Our lives are characterized by coming and going rather than staying and going deep. We live mostly on the surface. Much is left unsaid. So much is unknown. We share successes and joys but hide our struggles and failures and fears. We hurry through complicated lives, full of human interactions, but remain very much alone.

"There should be nothing in your life that someone doesn't know." It was fifteen years ago that I first heard those words, and I have no idea what the rest of my pastor's sermon was about. But that single sentence haunted me for years. I tried to forget it.

But not too long after we formed the Table, I finally got up the nerve to do something in response. I called a good friend, Matt. I told him that I would write down everything in my life I'd never confessed to anyone. I then asked him whether, after I'd completed my list to the best of my recollection, we could get together, so I could read my list to him and discuss it. He said, "Okay."

I braced myself for the task ahead. It was going to be forty years of things I'd kept hidden: judgment and criticism, harsh words, lust, lies. I knew it would be brutal, so before we hung up, I asked Matt hopefully, "Could we maybe get together in a couple of days?" Unfortunately (or maybe fortunately), he wasn't going to be available for another seven. And I spent that entire week working on my list.

At one point during that stretch, I mentioned to a pastor friend what I was doing. We were standing around at church, talking. He encouraged me in the exercise and asked if we might pray together, right there in the breezeway. He put his hand on my shoulder and began by asking God that I might have "excellent recall, remembering everything, every detail." I wanted to punch him! But throughout that week, his prayer was answered. Much to my dismay, it seemed like every conversation with Jennifer, every conversation period, and every quiet moment too, surfaced yet another memory—and all of them generated yet another item for my list.

When Matt and I finally got together, we sat alone in the conference room in my office.

With my heart racing and my stomach twisting, we prayed. And I began reading through my list out loud, filling in details and answering questions. I remember it being so hard to look at Matt's eyes. But I remember feeling compelled to check them every so often too. Would I see rejection or acceptance, revulsion or brotherly love? We talked and prayed some more. It took about an hour. And at the end, Matt prayed about forgiveness.

Matt and I became even closer friends that day—because of vulnerability. And I walked out of that room a freer man than I was when I'd walked in. I consider that experience one of the great milestones of my life. Though I still struggle with fear and reluctance when confessing things to my brothers, it's not as hard as it was before, and I'm able to do it more often.

"Almost all of us have spent nearly all of our lives feeling only partially safe, if at all," wrote Scott Peck. "Seldom, if ever, have we felt completely free to be ourselves."[15] How many men in trouble at work, or with a marriage under pressure, or caught in addiction to pornography or alcohol or something else, feel comfortable calling out to friends for rescue? How many men are willing to be honest about how the darkness of this world affects them? Oppresses them? I'll tell you how many. Very few.

Most of us, if we sense someone pushing in, leaning in, trying to see the real us, we change the subject. We make our polite escapes. We order our lives to fend people off. We keep busy so that we don't have time for deep-hearted friendships.

That's why most men's attempts at community fail. We want to be rescued. Deep down and desperately, we yearn for life and freedom as strongly as we yearn for anything else. "Most of the time, though," Peck wrote, "this thrust, this energy, is enchained by fear, neutralized by defenses and resistances."[16] Because we're afraid, we remain stuck in the darkness of our predicaments.

But honesty and vulnerability aren't weakness. Being willing to risk them is precisely the opposite. "It's courage beyond measure," wrote Brené Brown. It's courageous to face our brokenness head-on. It's brave to try to get better—both for us and for the people in our lives. It's daring to do the work necessary to grow and learn how to hurt the people we love (and ourselves) less. Honesty and vulnerability are actually *the* hallmarks of true masculine courage.

Mercy is another.

Jesus is always disruptive. His rescues, while desperately needed, shake up our lives in all the best ways—and for our own good. And he often works his disruption through our friends. This makes for messy and uncomfortable interactions, painful ones even. "Iron sharpens iron, and one man sharpens another" (Prov. 27:17).

He'll create groups full of bothersome and broken people, unexpected men with eccentric quirks, because those kinds of groups are the ones that can help us become less broken ourselves. We're sure to like some of the people he brings, of course. Very much. But others, inevitably, we'll like less so. They'll have different ways of doing things, different senses of humor, different politics. They'll annoy and provoke and might even wound us—and we're sure to do the same to them.

"These frets and rubs," though, wrote the long-shadowed C. S. Lewis, "are beneficial."[17] The differences and difficulties, the things we'd like to fix in our brothers, are often the very things God uses to expose where *we're* wounded and need healing. And vice versa. Being in close proximity to one another brings our limitations, insecurities, biases, jealousies, and even our cruelties into sharp focus. Community offers an opportunity to confront these things in ourselves. To overcome them. To heal.

And as we heal, we inevitably realize that we aren't as different as we thought, that we actually share many or most of the same fears and struggles. We realize that we're all in this thing together. That we are, all of us, broken. That we're all in desperate need of rescue.

As we heal and mature, we become, as the Anabaptist anti-Nazi Eberhard Arnold wrote, "reconciled to people's imperfection."[18] Reconciled even to our own. And then, finally, we begin to get a whole lot better at being kind and loving toward other people and ourselves—and *that* opens up to us an entirely new kind of life.

If you're curious about what that means—*an entirely new kind of life*—then keep reading, my friend. Getting there is what chapter 5 is all about. There's much good ahead.

– CLIP IN –
"TRUSTFUL"
004

The assumption that community is increasingly hard to find is well founded," wrote Parker Palmer. "It is difficult to find or create relationships of duration and reliability in our kind of world."[19]

Our fast-paced, compartmentalized lives and our mixed-up, self-oriented priorities make the establishment of authentic communities very nearly impossible—unless, that is, we trust God enough to allow *him* to muster the right men, to build those kinds of relationships on our behalf.

Brother, we need to trust him.

> For my thoughts are not your thoughts,
>> neither are your ways my ways, declares the
>> Lord.
> For as the heavens are higher than the earth,
>> so are my ways higher than your ways
>> and my thoughts than your thoughts.
>> (Isa. 55:8–9)

Consider these questions and capture your responses in a journal or a notes app on your phone.

004.1   What struck you about this chapter or in the story of the sub rescue? Pull out a pen or pencil or your phone and describe whatever stood out to you personally.

004.2   Are you surprised by this approach to community? How do you feel about surrendering control to God of who is in your rescue team? Circle a number below:

<< I AM VERY COMFORTABLE WITH IT - - I AM NOT COMFORTABLE AT ALL >>
1   2   3   4   5   6   7   8   9   10

Whatever number you've chosen, write several sentences explaining why you've chosen it. Know that raw honesty is much more important than saying some "right" thing. God craves your honesty, and he can handle anything you can hurl at him.

004.3   What criteria would you use to select your rescue team members if you were going to do it all by yourself? Make as complete a list as possible. And, again, being honest is essential. Don't list a bunch of religiously acceptable answers. Capture the criteria that you'd honestly use if it were up to you.

Experiment with listening prayer. Find a place where you can sit comfortably for twenty to thirty minutes, a place you're unlikely to be interrupted. Ask the Holy Spirit to direct your thoughts. Pray against distraction, against fatigue, against confusion.

Then, simply remain quiet for a length of time. Whatever feels appropriate. Just breathe and relax. Enjoy a few moments of solitude. And when you're ready, ask God this question: *What are the qualities I should be looking for and valuing in the members of my rescue team?*

Now, sit quietly for ten to twenty minutes. Again, don't feel pressured to hear anything. And don't rush it. Listen with your heart. Be aware of what thoughts come. Listen for that inner voice. When you're done, in one or two sentences, describe whatever words or ideas or pictures came to mind.

Pray right now.

*Jesus, I want to live the kind of life you make possible.
I want to be in community. I want to be connected—
to belong. I want to be part of a rescue team. But I'm
going to need your help. I want you to gather the right
men. I want you to gather to me the men you've chosen
for me according to your criteria, not my own. Bring
men who can become my true brothers.*

    I trust you. Help me to trust you more.

    Amen.

Now, **relax**. "My suggestion, just based on personal experience," wrote David Dusek, founder of Rough Cut Men Ministries, "is to pray hard for God to bring the right person into your life.... Then, just keep doing what you're doing."[20] Sit back and let God work. Wait with eager expectation and an open heart.

Be forewarned, though, that the group that forms around you might look nothing like you expect. Often the people God wants to bless you with (and the people he wants to bless *through you*) are not those you would choose. He might pull together a group as seemingly ragtag as those twelve Jesus gathered to himself. And that would be an excellent thing. The groups we create ourselves, based on worldly criteria, aren't typically worth our time, not when compared to the groups God creates for us. Those groups, though, are worth everything.

HOLD US TOGETHER

And love will hold us together
Make us a shelter to weather the storm
And I'll be my brother's keeper
So the whole world will know that we're not alone

// Matt Maher, songwriter

SAWS AND TORCHES AND DEVOTION

The Bridger Hotshots are in the middle of a roll—a blistering, fourteen-day stretch of sixteen-plus-hour days fighting a wildland fire. The crew is based in the Jackson Ranger District of the Bridger-Teton National Forest in Wyoming. Right now, though, they're miles to the northeast, halfway across the state, the only hotshot crew fighting a medium-sized fire in Bighorn National Forest.

What's being called the Bucking Mule Fire was discovered in the Bucking Mule Falls area six days ago. Experts suspect that it was started by downed power lines. When the hotshots got assigned to it, the fire was less than a hundred acres in size. But it's made some impressive runs recently and has now torn through more than forty-five hundred acres. The area is remote, full of steep mountains and deep gorges and thick expanses of lodgepole pine.

Mountain pine beetles have aided and abetted this destruction. The beetles get under the bark of lodgepole pines and eventually kill them. These beetles have devastated forests in all nineteen western states and Canada, destroying more than ninety million acres with unbelievable kill rates. In the Bucking Mule Falls area, they've killed more than 90 percent of the lodgepoles, leaving the hillsides and mountainsides full of dead, dry wood. Perfect fuel for forest fires. On top of that, hundreds of miles of power lines run through the area. And when those zombie trees fall, they sometimes break those lines, providing the spark needed to light all that kindling.

But that's not all. Bighorn National Forest is currently under a red flag, a warning issued by the National Weather Service when weather conditions become ideal for wildland fires: when vegetation is dry, relative humidity is low, air temperatures are high, and winds are strong. Bighorn has been under intermittent red flag warnings for much of the summer. Current gusts are up to forty and fifty miles per hour.

The prevailing winds in the area during the summer months are southwesterly, blowing to the northeast. But the Bridger Hotshots have been fighting for days to contain the eastern edge of the Bucking Mule Fire, since winds recently have been blowing more east than north. Weary from long, demanding shifts, it's taking a lot of willpower for these guys to get out of their sleeping bags in the mornings. Today, though, the winds shifted, and the team has relocated to the north edge, where the fire is threatening a historic lodge and a set of cabins.

The hotshots arrived to the site of their new assignment in the late morning and in a billow of dust. When they showed up at the lodge, two smoke jumpers were already there leading the charge, along with two Forest Service engine crews. They had all been working on getting everything in place before the fire arrives—laying hoses and getting sprinklers and pumps set—all to protect the main structure and its surrounding cabins.

Aaron Wright is the superintendent of the Bridger Hotshots. The first thing he does upon arrival is to get an update from the engine crew captains. He scans the mountains as they talk. "We don't expect the fire to be here today," one of the captains offers.

Wright, eyes still on the ridges to the south. "Hmm, I don't know. It seems pretty close to me." He thinks about how fast the winds have been shoving the fire forward. "I've been wrestling this fire for a few days now, and I think there's a good chance it gets here late this afternoon or evening."

"I think you're right." An older man walks up to the gathered group. Wright turns. It's Bill Torres, an experienced smoke jumper and an old friend.

"Hey, Bill. It's good to see you, brother. This thing's really starting to smoke."

At that moment, Wright notices another man. He's standing off at a distance but listening intently to their conversation—and he's not in uniform. One of the engine captains, anticipating the question, explains that the man is the lodge's caretaker.

"His name is Kyle Turner," the captain says. "He grew up here, and he's decided to defy our evacuation order. He was here when we got here, handling those garden hoses. He's a good dude. He and his wife and their two young daughters live in one of them cabins."

Wright gives the two captains additional directions, focusing them on the most important buildings. He and Torres then walk over and have a short conversation with Turner. Then Wright invites the old jumper to come with him to address his hotshots. The two men approach nineteen other men gathered around the ten-person crew-carrier trucks, which they call "the buggies." The guys are talking in hushed tones, preparing for battle. Pulling tools and gear out of the vehicles. Topping up fuel and oil for the chainsaws. Checking backpacks. Filling water bottles. Chugging water.

"All right, gentlemen," Wright says. "Some of you know Bill Torres. He's one of the finest jumpers in the Forest Service. He and I think this fire is coming this way and fast. And these are historic buildings, which we want to keep from burning. But here's something else: the guy setting up hoses over there is named Kyle. He and his wife live here with their two daughters, aged eight and eleven. That's their cabin right over there. That one. He could have evacuated. He definitely *should* have evacuated."

Laughter ripples through the men.

"But," Wright continues, "we're gonna help this dad save his family's home."

The men answer with another ripple of "uh-huh" and "yes, sir" and "yeah, Supe."

Wright nods. "As you guys know, this fire of ours has plenty of fuel and plenty of wind. It's been crowning every day since we've been here, so there's no way we're going to hold it here. No matter what we do, it'll jump and dodge any lines we make on this end. So we're not going to worry about that right now. We'll chase her down later. What we *are* going to worry about is saving these structures. It's going to be close, but I think we can get it done."

"So here's what we're going to do," Wright continues. "We're going to cut a nice long fire line between us and that mountain. Then we're going to do a burnout and widen that break as much as we can. We're going to steal as much fuel on the other side of that line as we can, as far up that pitch as possible, before the fire can get at it."

The hotshots look from their beloved leader to the mountain. An eighty-foot-thick carpet of dead trees covers the slope from base to ridge. However this thing turns out, it's going to be quite a show.

"Let's get to work."

Fire suppression is a challenging and complicated thing. No two fires are the same. The basic principles, though, are always pretty simple. Fire needs three things to burn: heat, fuel, and oxygen. Therefore, to contain the spread of any fire, firefighters must find a way to remove one or more of those elements. Because of the scale of fires they typically face, hotshots often try to remove the second: fuel. To do this, they use fire lines.

Fire lines act as walls, in a sense, because they contain a fire's spread, but they are actually the opposite; they are voids. Buffer zones where all combustible material has been removed—all the way from massive trees down to tiny twigs and leaves. Fire lines starve a fire of fuel and work to slow or redirect its movement. They can even stop a fire outright.

Firefighters make use of natural fire lines whenever they can: rivers, lakes, rocky slopes, plowed fields, roads. But when they need to, they'll create their own. And that's what the Bridger Hotshots are about to do.

Twenty men in hard hats, green Nomex pants, and yellow Nomex shirts grab their tools and begin moving like a well-oiled machine. (Nomex is a durable synthetic material that's flame and heat resistant to more than 500 degrees Fahrenheit.) They approach the place where Superintendent Wright wants the fire line, spread out, and get to work cutting and scraping.

Fire lines typically have two parts: the cut and the scrape. The parts run parallel to each other but perpendicular to the approach of fire. The *cut* is where hand crews remove all flammable surface material—trees, stumps, downed logs, shrubs, brush, grasses. It's usually twenty to thirty feet wide, wide enough to divert a fire's forward momentum.

A *scrape* is more narrow and is placed on the cut's far side, away from the fire. It's a one- to three-foot strip where hand crews not only remove surface materials but dig out anything below the surface too, all the way down to mineral soil. This prevents the fire from spreading through roots, duff, and other subsurface fuel.

Hand crews use shovels, axes, and chainsaws to do their work, but they utilize some custom tools too: the Pulaski, a combination ax and mattock, which allows firefighters to chop trees and limbs and also dig and scrape; and the McLeod, which is combo rake and hoe, with coarse tines on one side and a sharpened blade on the other. It's designed to rake fire lines and cut branches and roots. Who uses what depends on the various roles. Sawyers do the cutting. Swampers clear brush and whatever's been cut. Diggers do the digging.

Sometimes, when fires are big and driven by fierce winds, fire lines need to be even wider than thirty feet. So to widen them, hotshots will use the very thing they are fighting. They'll start their own fires, because fire can eliminate flammable materials more quickly than men with hand tools. To do this, hotshots use drip torches: handheld canisters that drip burning fuel, a mixture of diesel and gasoline. They'll walk an existing fire line, drip torches in hand, lighting the grass and brush that sits between the line and the approaching fire. This is called a "burnout."

THE GRANITE MOUNTAIN HOTSHOTS CONDUCTING A BURNOUT
OPERATION DURING THE WHITEWATER-BALDY COMPLEX
FIRE IN THE GILA NATIONAL FOREST IN NEW MEXICO

After cutting and scraping a line between the lodge complex and the mountain, the Bridger Hotshots begin their burnout operation. Because of the dry conditions, things get going quickly. In just a few minutes, the burnout starts to run up the underbrush and *whoosh* into that carpet of dead lodgepoles.

"Supe" Wright is working next to Cole Clayton, the newest and youngest member of the team. Watching the inferno grow, he turns. "Cole," he says, "you're gonna be telling stories about this day for a very long time. Right now, you're facing down a major crown fire while generating another fire to burn up into it. This, son, is going to be something to remember."

When the burnout is going the way they intended, Wright lets out a loud *hoot*. It's time to pull back. Hoots echo back up and down the line through the smoke. Their faces blackened with soot and their clothes soaked through with sweat, the hotshots pull back to the lodge complex and gather everyone to the safety of a large green field that sits in front of the main lodge building. Everyone is quiet as they watch the burn show.

The main fire generates a massive column of smoke. Because of the wind, the smoke is beginning to lie right over the captivated company. The smoke from the burnout then starts to contribute to it, getting sucked into the updrafts of the column. And then the fires meet, right at the top of the ridge, and it's like everything in the world is burning all at once. It's the most terrible and magnificent fire display any of them has seen this close up—even Wright and Torres. The flames grow to a height of at least three hundred feet. The sound is truly impressive too, like that of a speeding freight train.

And then it's all over. Everything burns so hot and so fast that, in a couple of hours, the entire slope is black with bare sticks standing and only a few wisps of smoke curling toward the sky. The fire didn't touch the structures—not the lodge, not the cabins—not Kyle's family's cabin. There are smiles and fist bumps all around. For one of the men there that day, though, there are tears of deep gratitude too.

A fire like the fictional Bucking Mule Fire I just described is small compared to the Great Fire of 1910, which is still the largest forest fire in United States history. A dry winter that year, followed by hurricane-force winds over two days in mid-August, caused thousands of smaller wildfires to converge into one massive firestorm.

The Big Blowup, as it's come to be called, burned three million acres of forest in Montana, Idaho, Washington, and British Columbia. The blaze killed eighty-five people (seventy-eight of them firefighters) and consumed countless homes and buildings—as well as several small towns—before rain and snow slowed the horrifying conflagration.

WALLACE, IDAHO, REBUILDING AFTER THE GREAT FIRE OF 1910

At that time, the US Forest Service was brand new, and its survival as a federal agency was nowhere near guaranteed. It had been in existence for only five years when the Big Blowup ignited, and it had been struggling for funding. The Great Fire built public and congressional support, though, and solidified its mission: to fight and suppress every wildfire at all costs.

By 1935, the agency had adopted the "10:00 a.m. rule," which mandated that all fires be brought under control by ten o'clock the morning *after* they were spotted. The thinking being that, typically, up until 10:00 a.m. weather conditions favor the firefighters; after 10:00 a.m., though, they favor the fire. According to Brendan McDonough, a former Granite Mountain hotshot, the afternoons are "when you really earn your money."[1]

The effect of the 10:00 a.m. rule was positive—until it wasn't. For many years, the policy prevented fires from blowing up as the Great Fire did. But over time, the absence of fire from our forests changed them. The strict policy created dense forests with floors piled high with fuel. The policy, paradoxically, ultimately *increased* rather than decreased the likelihood and prevalence of catastrophic blazes.

Today, five federal agencies—the Forest Service, the Bureau of Land Management, the Bureau of Indian Affairs, the National Park Service, and the US Fish and Wildlife Service—and state and local fire departments work together to manage wildland fires. Coordinated by the National Interagency Fire Center (NIFC) in Boise, Idaho, these agencies deploy wildland firefighting resources with a more balanced approach.

Firefighter safety and public safety are their priorities, but they also recognize the role of wildland fire as an essential ecological process. Therefore, the folks at the NIFC let some fires run their course and control and suppress others, especially those that threaten human lives, homes, or businesses.

The various teams available to federal, state, and local agencies are engine crews, type 2 hand crews, smoke jumpers, helitack crews, aircrews that fly helicopters adapted to carry water buckets, and air tanker crews who fly specially designed aircraft that can drop massive amounts of fire-retardant foams and gels.

And, of course, they have the hotshots.

Hotshot crews are the elite infantry forces of the firefighting world. They deploy on foot into hostile environments. They're highly trained, well-equipped, super-fit, and proficient in all manner of fire-suppression tactics. They carry lots of gear and can live and work and hike in the wilderness for weeks. These guys are comfortable being uncomfortable. It's brutal, heroic work.

"In their way," wrote author and journalist John Maclean, "hotshots are as elite as smoke jumpers, capable of battling fire anywhere at any time, but unlike jumpers they specialize in big fires requiring teamwork."[2] They work in twenty- to twenty-two-person teams and operate with military precision in high-stress environments. They are led by a superintendent, one or two assistant superintendents, and two or three squad leaders.

"Unlike smoke jumpers, the twenty members of a hotshot crew stay together all season, often year after year," wrote Maclean. "They work, eat, sleep, shower and take time off as a unit—and when trouble strikes, they stick together."[3]

The first hotshot crews were established in the 1940s in Southern California in the Cleveland and Angeles National Forests—"put together as an alternative to recruiting in saloons."[4] They were so named because they got closer to the heat and the fire than anyone else. Today, there are more than one hundred interagency hotshot crews, most of them scattered across the fire-prone West.

Why do wildland firefighters do what they do? Annette O'Doan, public information officer for the US Forest Service and former hotshot herself, explained that it's all about "saving people and saving the land."[5]

Bucking Mule Falls

Approaching Fire

Fisher Mountain Log & Cabins

Fisher Mountain

Big Horn Mountains
Northern Rockies

AREA BURNED: 4,500 ACRES
WINDS: GUSTING UP TO 50 MILES PER HOUR
PERCENT OF FIRE CONTAINED: 10%

S
E W
N

BELiEF:

I'M WAY TOO BUSY.

Do you ever think, *All the religion I need is church on Sundays. Okay, maybe I'll drop into a men's group every once in a while or go to the men's retreat next year. Anything more than that, though, would be too much. I'm slammed with work and family obligations. I don't have any extra capacity. Plus, having other guys in my life has never been a priority for me. Some guys need it, but I just don't.*

This kind of thinking is rooted neither in truth nor in the goodness of God. *Think again.*

One of the significant differences between heaven and earth is love. We take it a lot less seriously than God does. There's so much we don't know about him. He's infinite and infinitely mysterious. But we do know this: love is at the core of everything God is and everything he does.

"Love is from God," wrote the apostle John (1 John 4:7). He even wrote, "God *is* love" (1 John 4:8).[6] He personifies it. You see, while God is a person unto himself, he's also actually, as Dallas Willard wrote, "a sweet society of Persons: Father, Son, and Holy Spirit."[7] His very nature is that of a community of love—a corps of three persons who bestow unsparingly upon one another a deep and never-ending love.

God's kind of love, therefore, is the communal kind. The mutual kind. It demands *another*. In his kind of love, someone loves someone else. God loves Jesus. God loves the Holy Spirit. They both love him back (and each other). But that's not all. He also created beings—people— beyond this tight community of three. Lots of *anothers*. And because God loves us, you and me, "in the same way" that he loves Jesus, he invites us, too, into his sweet society (John 17:23).[8] He invites us to participate in his community of boundless love. He invites us into his *family*.

But even that's not all. When we come into God's family, he helps us to participate *as* family members. He fills us with his love and empowers us to love others. He pours love into each of us so that we can experience and enjoy it, for sure, but also so that it overflows. So that we, in turn, can love him back, and so that we can love other people too—other *anothers*. He offers us all more than we can handle, so we can have plenty of love to give away.

His intention, his dream, is that this family of love grows and grows. It's his great desire that all of his sons and daughters love each other just like he does. "A new commandment I give to you," Jesus said, "that you love one another: just as I have loved you, you also are to love one another" (John 13:34). Nothing else in the world matters to him as much. Love, therefore, is our number one priority. "Above all," wrote Peter, "keep loving one another earnestly" (1 Pet. 4:8). "Let all that you do be done in love," added Paul (1 Cor. 16:14).

When all the blare and babble of this world recedes, we discover that these lives of ours are about one thing: *love.* Our every moment. Every decision. Every action. Every interaction. Everything about our existence. All of them—somehow, someway—are about love.

Love isn't something to be experienced intellectually. We don't encounter it by contemplating it. We don't enjoy love or express it with pleasant thoughts or best wishes or "good vibes." Nor is love merely a feeling. Genuine love is active. It happens when someone *acts* for the benefit of another person. Genuine love is embodied in flesh and blood. Breath and mud.

A private or individualistic faith in Jesus is a myth. An intellectual Christianity isn't a thing. Christianity is a religion-at-work. It's a religion-at-love. "There is no other form for the Christian life except a common one," wrote that religious original Richard Rohr.[9] No one should ever *read* Scripture without also *living* Scripture, and living Scripture means living in community. Jesus said, "Whoever believes in me will also do the works that I do" (John 14:12). And what he did was get in close and love with vigor.

This is foreign thinking for some men, and it may be hard to hear. (It was for me.) It requires some rewiring. We're a busy generation. There is never enough time to accomplish what we want to, which is, for most of us, to build impressive careers and splendid families. For most of us, therefore, community is something to fit in when it's convenient. We like community, but on the side—and not too much.

If we ever desire connection and belonging, joy and peace, we'd prefer to just buy them—clean, quick, efficient. But it doesn't work like that. Authentic community is never clean or quick or efficient. And it isn't a commodity, like an occasional golf vacation or an annual ski trip with the guys. You can't get it by sporadically dropping in at a monthly men's event or by simply attending your church's annual men's summit.

Community isn't a product; it's a *by-product*. "Whoever does the will of God," Jesus said, "he is my brother and sister and mother" (Mark 3:35). And the will of God is, of course, love. Therefore, community forms—*family forms*—as a *by-product* of loving. Community forms as we turn our care and attention away from ourselves and toward other people.

When we do that, something shocking happens. We immediately begin getting access to the *benefits* of community. Those things we've been chasing—connection, belonging, purpose, significance, joy, peace, even healing—they start flooding into our lives. When we stop trying to grasp for them by grasping at material things, through achievement and accumulation, self-help and leadership books, substances and distractions, and instead focus on the needs of other people, we begin getting what we've always wanted. By doing what Jesus said: by targeting love, we receive what we've always needed.

Authentic community is never about anything but love. It has no other aim. Authentic community isn't about networking. It isn't about business, political, intellectual, or philanthropic goals. Members are sure to be healed and encouraged by the fact of being in community. They are sure to be emboldened to go and do things outside the community. But the focus of any particular community should always be the community itself—and God, of course. The goals should be to build deeper relationships, create stronger unity, and foster more love.

Many men will shift uncomfortably at the mention of love in the context of masculine communities. But to leave love out of a book about community would be ridiculous. Without love, community isn't even possible, even among men, even among very tough men. Love isn't optional. It's the essential element. Community will never even begin to form unless and until two or more people start loving one another enough.

Okay, so what is that? What's *enough*?

That's another question that's hard to answer with any kind of specificity. Our personalities and circumstances are complex and different. The problem is made even more difficult because of how much mystery surrounds the power that creates and maintains community. What we can say with certainty, though, is that it's *a lot*.

How do we know that? Well, we have a benchmark. It's Jesus, and he set the mark high. For love, for family, for community, he sacrificed everything.

Christ Jesus, who, though he was in the form of God, did not count equality with God a thing to be grasped, but emptied himself, by taking the form of a servant, being born in the likeness of men. And being found in human form, he humbled himself by becoming obedient to the point of death, even death on a cross. (Phil. 2:5–8)

Jesus laid down his life. He sacrificed himself for all humanity. He showed us exactly what it means to be part of God's family. He showed what kind of love real community requires: a robust, *all-in, all-the-way-to-the-end* kind of love.

And that kind of love is a courageous, masculine kind. It's not the kind that should make any man uncomfortable. It's the kind of love shared and extended by men of a certain character and sense of duty. Members of alpine search-and-rescue teams who risk their lives in harsh weather at high altitudes. Coast Guard rescue swimmers who dive selflessly into cold and churning seas. Members of interagency hotshot teams who stand in front of unfathomable flames. It's the kind of love that faces grave risks so that others may live.

It's the kind of love that drove William Cummings to *volunteer* to go to Bataan. Thinking only of the poor souls who would soon face some of the most horrific moments of World War II, he convinced a skeptical Army to let him go. "I'm sure that they need me there," he declared.[10]

"In the end," wrote author and editor Charles Moore, "it's a matter of whether we will lay down our lives for one another."[11] Jesus modeled that kind of love. He set the standard and calls us to meet it. "This is my commandment," he said, "that you love one another as I have loved you" (John 15:12). "He laid down his life for us," wrote John, "and we ought to lay down our lives for the brothers" (1 John 3:16).

Firefighters do what they do for various reasons. Chief among them, of course, is to earn a living for themselves and to provide for their families. But another is duty. "Someone has to fight the flames," wrote Brendan McDonough.[12] Someone has to help manage the land and preserve our natural resources. But someone has to protect the rest of us.

The stated mission of the Jackson Hotshots is "to protect life, property and resources threatened by wildland fires."[13] And they and other brave men and women go out there and do just that, despite the cost. You put "the mission above yourself and your comforts to get the job done, because that's what needs to be done," explained Adam Hernandez, a former captain of the Kings River Hotshots.[14]

Federal agencies employ more than ten thousand wildland firefighters. During fire season, they spend hours, days, weeks, months in harm's way, facing and fighting the raging infernos that would otherwise destroy lives and families and homes and communities.

> "I am sure every crew says the same thing, we strive to be the best shot crew in the nation.... We try to get where we're the most helpful. Try to work our way into those spots where we feel like we can make the biggest difference."[15]
> —Dan Pickard, superintendent of the Entiat Hotshots

Our modern world is super-complex. We're connected to lots of people in lots of different places in lots of different ways. So to whom should we devote *ourselves*? To whom should we share *our all-in, all-the-way-to-the-end* love?

Indeed, reasonably quickly, we all run into the fact that we're finite beings living finite lives. There are only so many hours in a day. Our time is scarce. We have only so much capacity to love before we exhaust ourselves, before we reach the human limits of our time, physical energy, and emotional capacity.

Only Jesus could love every person in the world. Only he could lay down his life for everyone. Once again, he is God, and we are not. Facing usual human constraints, we can know and love and sacrifice our lives for relatively few. We can share at the required depth with only a few people. Even if we narrowed our focus to just the people in our neighborhoods, or at places of work, or even just the people who attend our churches, it wouldn't be enough. We couldn't possibly make all of those people top priorities in our lives. There would still be too many.

We can certainly try to act in *loving ways* toward all of those people—and everyone we meet. And we should do that. (I need to do it better.) But we can't possibly hope to give our *all-in, all-the-way-to-the-end* love to all of them. That's why King Solomon distinguished friends and *true friends*, between acquaintances and *brothers*. He wrote about a certain kind of friend, one "who sticks closer than a brother" (Prov. 18:24).

Friends who stick closer than a brother. The wise king was talking about rescue teams.

Near his death, Saint Francis of Assisi prayed over his fellow friars: "I have done what is mine to do. May Christ teach you what is yours."[16] He might have also prayed, "I have loved the people who were mine to love. The people, God, whom you gave to me to love deeply."

Who are *your people*? Who are the men you would die for?

Answering these questions sometimes requires finding new people—people we don't yet know. Much more often, though, the answers are found by surrendering into deep relationship with the people who are already in our lives.

An older and wiser man once told me that the best evidence that we are where God wants us to be is that we are there. God is powerful and good. Though we cannot see it, we can trust that God has been, and still is, at work in our lives—busily at work. We can trust that he's given us specific experiences, put us in certain geographic places, placed us in physical and virtual proximity with particular people because he wants us to love them, truly and intensely. We must, therefore, begin to view our surroundings differently. We must look at the people surrounding our lives with new eyes.

Because of his goodness and love, we can trust that God is, right now, calling us into community. We can trust that he is, at this very moment, whispering into the hearts of some few men—*about us*. We can trust that he's forming for us a rescue team: a community of friends who'll stick with us closer than brothers.

"Find like-hearted kings living in the same
direction. Sign treaties. When they are at
war, you are at war."[17] —Dan Allender

And then, when we *do* start finding those men—even one man—we've got to trust that our job is simply to commit to them. To lean in. To invest. Thomas Merton wrote, "Our job—one of our big responsibilities—is to build community in any way we can."[18] Our job is to *love*—to be supremely concerned for our brothers, those new and those long known. Our job is to begin noticing what our friends need and considering how God might want to use us to address those needs.

Our job is to stand together in love and solidarity against the darkness.

The call is clear, and the bar is high. Jesus calls us to make our brothers, the members of our rescue teams, a high priority. We are to treat them like family but closer. Closer than brothers. This means nudging them a few notches higher on our daily priority lists than where they probably sit right now.

For rescue teams cannot exist at the edges of our lives. They must be front and center. Unity requires it. To be a member of one such team requires that we pull barriers down. It requires that we, as Charles Moore wrote, "make concerted choices to forgo some of our freedom, so that others can more naturally be in, and not just around, our lives."[19]

The closer-than-brothers standard requires that we make ourselves available to one another. That we make room for one another in our busy lives. It means frequent and regular involvement. It means commitment and patience and time.

If we want membership in a rescue team, we've got to be willing to take calls in the middle of the night. To answer emergency texts in the middle of our busy days. To stand beside men facing situations or decisions that are too hard or too scary for any man to face alone. We've got to get to the place where we're willing to give our brothers a couch to crash on, a shoulder to lean on, maybe even money to survive on.

The closer-than-brothers standard requires that we make the men in our communities our priorities to such an extent that other good things get crowded out. "We will have to form new lifestyle habits," wrote Moore, "and dispense with old patterns of living and thinking."[20] Being in authentic community requires that we begin to give up our old, selfish, self-centered striving and start *living* for the men of our teams.

Even in times when no crisis is at hand, we have to start showing up. When our brothers need prayer, when they need friendship, when they need a favor, when they need a sounding board, when they need wisdom, we've got to start showing up. We have to start checking in when we haven't heard anything for a while, be willing to grab coffee even when we're busy. We have to be willing to ask questions that are uncomfortable: "What are you *really* struggling with?" and "How is that struggle *really* going … *today?*"

The closer-than-brothers standard also requires loyalty, even when the going gets tough. It means recognizing and accepting that once we're in, we're in. It means sticking with brothers even when the relationships prove hard, maybe because of personal chemistry or maybe because one of them is in the midst of a personal crisis that makes him difficult to love. Even when people frustrate us or let us down, love requires that we stay.*

Rescue teams are rare and unusual in this dark world, and they don't form easily. If authentic community is something you want, you are going to have to contend for it. Being a part of a Jesus-inspired, Holy Spirit–energized rescue team requires courage: the courage to let God help us do what we cannot. It means summoning the bravery to let God guide us to the cross and help us become new men with new priorities. It means allowing God to rewire our thinking: to help us stop making excuses and start making time.

---

* There are times when separation is appropriate, of course. Those will be discussed in chapter 6.

If you want this, you must let God teach you to sacrifice, because being a part of a rescue team means going some places at the expense of others. It means spending time with some people to the temporary exclusion of others. It means being there for a brother in crisis and pushing off that round of golf or that trip to the gym. It can mean rescheduling that work lunch. A few times, it will probably even mean missing a family dinner or two—to be there for a brother in need.

Spending so much time together under harsh and trying conditions, hotshot crews become close. "The sense of camaraderie and family that is forged on a hotshot crew is that above any other unit in our industry," said Shawn Borgen, superintendent of the Flathead Hotshots. "We spend every waking minute together engaged, protecting each other, watching out for each other's safety."[21]

SMITH RIVER HOTSHOTS CUT A FIRE LINE WHILE FIGHTING THE
CEDAR FIRE IN SEQUOIA NATIONAL FOREST IN CALIFORNIA

Looking back on his experiences with the Granite Mountain Hotshots, Brendan McDonough wrote that his comrades "depended on each other for their lives and … would sacrifice everything for the next man."[22] And they weren't shy about how they thought about and acted toward one another, either. "Not only did they care about each other," wrote McDonough, "they talked about it openly."[23]

That spirit of love and honor and sacrifice is one of the prime things that makes hotshot crews so powerful. It makes them surprisingly effective against their terrible and unpredictable foe. Twenty or so people armed only with hand tools might seem poorly matched against massive, raging wildfires, but hotshot crews get called in because they can do a job and do it well. Working as one, they change the courses and slow the progress of massive wildland fires. And sometimes, they stop them right in their tracks.

Unity. Family.

Among the several things that surprised me about the men of the Cave was the extent to which they would offer each other (and me) their time and attention. I noticed a difference in the first few weeks after I'd joined. They had built an atmosphere of curiosity and commitment. It wasn't just the invitations to meet for breakfasts and lunches or to grab coffee. It was the volume of those invitations and the extent to which they accepted each other's invitations, especially when one of the group members was in some sort of crisis. But even when they weren't.

It wasn't just that they asked each other how they were doing. It was that they seemed to actually want to know. It was that they'd check in the next time we met and remember the details of what men had shared with them prior. They remembered week to week what people had asked for or prayed for or needed accountability for.

The night is long and dark. Evil abounds. The needs of the men and women living in our world are deep and dire. Because of the darkness, though, only a few men will ever allow themselves to hear God's call to community. But for those who do and for those who are daring enough to respond, the reward is tremendous.

> "The strength of the wolf is in the pack, the
> strength of the pack is in the wolf."[24]
> —Smith River Hotshots motto (quoting Rudyard Kipling)

When we start showing up for each other, when we have each other's backs, we gain something extraordinary. When we commit to showing up for one another no matter how busy or tired we are, when we commit to leaving no man behind, we gain something the darkness can never overcome. We gain life and goodness. Restoration and healing. Identity and acceptance. Answers and truth.

"Is it worth it?" asked Patrick Morley. "Absolutely."[25]

We also gain access to a place where we can meet God. Where we can deepen and purify and enrich our relationships with him. He is, after all, the first and most important member of any rescue team. When we spend time with our brothers, God is in our midst. That's why, for so many men, entering community is how we encounter him most often and most readily. It tends to be the most natural place for many men to worship, to pray, to hear his voice, to procure his wisdom, to face and overcome fears and failures, to find healing, and to celebrate his goodness.

The men and women profiled in the last verses of Acts chapter 2 offer a helpful and aspirational picture of authentic community. Scripture says they "devoted themselves to the apostles' teaching and the fellowship, to the breaking of bread and the prayers" (Acts 2:42). The Greek word used to describe their fellowship, *koinónia*, translates variously into "life together," "sharing in," "communion," "spiritual fellowship," and "a fellowship in the spirit."[26] They didn't meet rarely or sporadically.

They did life together. By loving one another, they became like family but closer.

How can we do the same with our brothers? What does brotherly love look like for modern men? What does it look like, practically, specifically, for us to be in community with the friends we've been given?

GOODWILL

In authentic community, we take time to get to know one another, hear each other's stories, and understand one another's experiences and motivations. We put each other's choices into those larger contexts. We try to put ourselves in each other's shoes—to understand things from each other's perspectives—and assume the best. We give our brothers the benefit of the doubt, assuming good intentions behind their actions.

We build empathy and compassion for our brothers. We are *for* them and want good things for them. "Love is not affectionate feeling," after all, wrote C. S. Lewis, "but a steady wish for the loved person's ultimate good as far as it can be obtained."[27]

HONOR

In authentic community, we honor one another. The apostle Paul challenged us to go big in this regard: to actually "outdo one another in showing honor" (Rom. 12:10). And that starts with humility. It starts by treating every brother in a rescue team with dignity, making it clear that they're worthy of love and belonging, worthy of time and attention. *Because they are.* "There are no ordinary people," wrote Lewis. "You have never talked to a mere mortal," he cautioned. "Next to the Blessed Sacrament itself, your neighbor is the holiest object presented to your senses."[28]

We honor our brothers by treating every person in our crew as important and essential. By valuing all personalities, all kinds of gifts and talents. By putting aside how culture categorizes people—how it considers some more worthy because of their backgrounds, achievements, socioeconomic statuses, appearances, whatever.

We honor our brothers by surrendering any feelings of superiority and recognizing that we're not the most important in the group, that our needs aren't superior. By being willing to hear the opinions of others, rather than forcing our own. By not demanding to be right or to have the last word. By sometimes taking the last place in line rather than rushing to be first. By taking less of something rather than grasping for more.

We honor our brothers by giving them our time. "Time," wrote Patrick Morley, "is *everything* to a relationship."[29] We take calls and answer voicemails and emails and texts. We honor one another also with our vulnerability. By being willing to communicate on a deep and personal level. By sharing the full extent of our stories and giving our brothers plenty of time to share their own. We honor one another with deep listening. By being curious and asking questions and checking in. By making thoughtful comments, remembering details like significant life events, quirks and preferences, likes and dislikes, dates and family members' names.

We honor our brothers by being willing to forgive them.

> Put on then, as God's chosen ones, holy and beloved, compassionate hearts, kindness, humility, meekness, and patience, bearing with one another and, if one has a complaint against another, forgiving each other; as the Lord has forgiven you, so you also must forgive. (Col. 3:12–13)

We *will* hurt each other at some point, and rescue teams can withstand that. What they usually can't withstand, though, are hard, unforgiving hearts.

SERVICE

In authentic community, we serve each other. "For freedom Christ has set us free," wrote the apostle Paul (Gal. 5:1). "Only do not use your freedom," he warned us, "as an opportunity for the flesh, but through love serve one another" (Gal. 5:13).

We serve our brothers by being alert to their needs and interested in their welfare. By noticing when a friend needs help. Or needs to talk. Or needs some compassion. Or needs wise counsel. Or needs to confess something. We serve our brothers when we notice that they need help but aren't asking for it, maybe because they don't know they need it or don't know that they can ask for it or are too embarrassed or too afraid of what it might do to the relationship if they do ask.

We serve our brothers by actually *doing* things. We shape our goodwill into good action—into real, physical manifestations of love and truth. Most times, those are relatively small. Sometimes a friend needs help with a project, needs a place to crash, needs help moving, needs an introduction, needs a referral, needs a recommendation, needs a sounding board as he wrestles with an upcoming decision.

But not all needs are small, of course. Sometimes a brother needs a rescue mission. All of us will, at some point, face the kind of fear and confusion and despair that come with the loss of a job, or a marriage, or our health, or a reputation. And then we get to walk right into the darkness and offer a brother a stretched-out hand—Jesus' hand of rescue. We get to be part of Jesus' saving work in the messy, human details of another man's life. "Stoop down and reach out to those who are oppressed," wrote Paul. "Share their burdens, and so complete Christ's law" (Gal. 6:2–3).[30]

Being a member of a rescue team means being willing to get our hands dirty and our feet wet. It means being ready to provide whatever service is required. It means being willing to offer spiritual companionship, our presence, our words, our material assistance, our lack of answers, our acceptance, our love.

One note must be made here. The descriptions of community in this chapter (and in the entire book, in fact) are aspirational. No group comes anywhere close to perfection. Though we're all growing in wholeness and holiness every day, we are sinful people living in a fallen world.

In every rescue team, there will be collisions of egos. There will be conflicts and misunderstandings. And that's okay. God works masterfully in the midst of those—to heal us, to help us become ever more whole and ever more holy. So we must be merciful toward ourselves and our brothers when we inevitably fall short. We are works in progress, as are our groups themselves. We will make mistakes. We will fail each other. And through those mistakes and failures, God will help us become better.

But the more goodwill and honor and service we put into our imperfect relationships, the better they get. The more we invest in our communities, the richer they become and the closer we get to reaching our aspirations. The more we notice and care, sacrifice and offer, the more our groups flourish. Christianity ignited and exploded when just a few people got serious about love.

It will again when *we* do. So let's get going.

In chapter 6, we roll up our sleeves and get practical.

– CLIP IN –
"DEVOTED"
005

Love is the most incredible gift we can give to another person. For those select few whom God sends into the orbits of our lives, creating authentic community together "is the best thing we can give them," wrote Thomas Merton.[31] Love is a force that emanates from beyond this world. Its light flows from heaven into our hearts and back out, into our dark world. When we love another, we direct the power of God into his or her life. It might not always seem like it, but nothing is better. Nothing is more potent than love. It's stronger than pain, stronger than fear, stronger than death. It *will* overcome this present darkness.

Consider these questions and capture your responses.

005.1   What struck you about this chapter or in the story of the Bridger Hotshots? Pull out a pen or pencil or your phone and describe whatever stood out to you personally.

005.2   What communities do you belong to? Spend a few minutes considering your loose-definition and narrow-definition communities. Make as complete a list as possible. Then make a second list. Write down the people in these communities with whom you are closest. List your dearest friends.

005.3   "Greater love has no one than this, that someone lay down his life for his friends" (John 15:13). How do you feel about Jesus' statement? What do you think about being called to *that* level of brotherly love? Circle a number below:

<< THAT SEEMS EXTREME - I'M FIRED UP! >>

1   2   3   4   5   6   7   8   9   10

Whatever number you've chosen, write a few sentences explaining why you chose it. Again, you have permission to be completely honest. As you write, make sure to imagine what this kind of devotion might mean for you and your daily living, practically.

005.4   How would you feel about having one or two or a few brothers for whom you would be willing to die? To whom you would become devoted, closer than brothers? Circle a number below:

<< I NEED TO THINK ABOUT THAT - - - - - - - - - - - - - I'M READY TO GO! >>

1   2   3   4   5   6   7   8   9   10

In a few sentences, capture your thoughts about the number you chose.

Now, because we're all finite beings and cannot do everything, consider how it would feel to have to say *no* to other commitments, other communities in your life, in favor of the rescue team to which God might be calling you. Would that change your previous answer? Circle a number below:

<< I NEED TO THINK ABOUT THAT - - - - - - - - - I'M STILL READY TO GO! >>

1   2   3   4   5   6   7   8   9   10

Again, jot down your thoughts about the number you chose.

005.5   Let's get really honest. Are you worried about whether God actually *does* have brothers in mind for you? Are you unsure that he's mustering a rescue team *for you*? Are you doubtful that he will come through?

<< Not doubtful at all - Very doubtful >>

1   2   3   4   5   6   7   8   9   10

Whatever number you circled, write several sentences explaining why you chose it. This is another question where raw honesty is essential, and simply saying the "right" things isn't important at all. Remember, God craves your honesty; he can handle it.

Experiment with listening prayer. Find a place where you can sit comfortably for twenty to thirty minutes, a place you're unlikely to be interrupted. Ask the Holy Spirit to direct your thoughts. Pray against distraction, against fatigue, against confusion.

Then, simply remain quiet for a length of time. Whatever feels right. Just breathe and relax. Enjoy a few moments of calm. And when you're ready, close your eyes and pray: *Jesus, I need your help. I need to sense your voice. I want to know your will. Please show me a face or two or three. Who do you have in mind for my rescue team? Is there someone I already know? Is there someone I've been turning away? Or, if not, where are you calling me?*

Now, sit quietly for ten to twenty minutes. Again, don't feel pressured to see specific things or hear particular names or think certain thoughts. Be open, and don't rush it. Listen with your heart. Listen for that inner voice. If you struggle to hear, don't sweat it. Don't dwell on it. Just try again later.

Also, remember, from our perspective, God is unpredictable. So having asked these questions, you might sense his answers in other contexts, even when you least expect them. For example, you might gain an answer in a moment of unguarded thought or in a conversation with a trusted friend.

When you do sense answers, though, make sure to write them down. Then, tuck those notes away, and before you act on them, go ahead and read the next and final chapter.

But right now, **pray**. Take just a moment before you move on.

> *Jesus, help me to have the courage to listen. Help me to sense and know where you're calling me. Help me to have the courage to go there, to love and invest in my brothers. Help me to trust you and trust them. Help me to love you and love them. Help me to find deep fellowship and communion with the people you've given to me and to whom I've been given.*
>
> *Amen.*

TO THE TABLE

Hear the voice of love that's calling
There's a chair that waits for you
And a Friend who understands
Everything you're going through

// Zach Williams et al., songwriters

BARS AND BIBLES AND CONFIDENCE

The inmate sits on the edge of his bunk, stunned.

It's true.

The man's bitter distrust. His furious cynicism. They've somehow faded, been replaced.

It's all true.

The man's name is Curtis, and his feet are planted flat on the hard floor, his elbows resting on his knees, his hands clasped together, looking straight ahead at a painted wall. His prison cell is so small that the light yellow surface is only about twelve inches away from his face. He's looked at that same paint and same concrete for so many years, but now it looks different to him. All of the walls, the bars. All of the stone, the steel. It *all* looks different.

What just happened? Whatever that was … it changes everything.

Nothing about his grim surroundings has changed, of course. It is him. *He's* changed. And he can feel it, and that feeling compels him to turn and look into a small plastic mirror attached by magnet to the steel frame of his bunk. He barely recognizes the face staring back through the scratches. It isn't filled with hate.

Curtis reaches for his Bible. He lifts it from atop a white five-gallon paint bucket, empty and upside down, his makeshift shelf. He holds it in both hands, feeling the weight of the pages and the texture of the cover beneath his calloused fingers. He grips it tight, subconsciously trying to get close to Jesus once again. One more time.

As he holds the book, he begins considering his life. His choices. His circumstances. He thinks about his crimes. His victims. His family. Rebekah. Shane. He sees them all differently than he ever has before. Gone is the hard heart that has caused so much pain for so many people. In its place is a new heart, one that allows him to feel things he's never really felt before—remorse. Empathy. A deeper love.

Jesus' presence. His promises. This peace. All of it. It's all true.

The feelings are intense. But at this point, he is all but cried out. So he just hugs the Bible to his chest and falls sideways onto the thin mattress, pulling his legs up onto the bunk. Feeling a bit foolish in that position, he thanks God that his cellmate won't be back from his mailroom job for a couple more hours. And he weeps quietly with what tears he has left after the deluge in the chapel. He is careful not to make noise, for the unwritten rules of this place are still deeply ingrained. *Show no weakness.*

He lies there for a minute. Then two. Then three. Thinking about the people he's hurt. Abandoned. The muscles in his stomach convulse gently as he sobs. Otherwise, though, he barely moves. He remains in this near-fetal position for a long time, overwhelmed by a crazy combination of surrender and peace, remorse and love. At some point, he begins to pray.

> *Thank you, Jesus. Thank you for loving someone like me. Thank you for dying for a man like me. I still can barely believe it. But I do believe. I believe that all of this is real. I know it is. I know that you are real. I know you can hear me. I know that you're here with me right now. And as crazy as it is, I know that I'm forgiven. That I am loved and free.*
>
> *. . .*

Please help me make things right. Please help me make up for the things I've done—for all the things I haven't done as a husband, father, son, grandson, brother. Help me, Jesus. As best I can, help me to make things right.

...

And help me tell my brothers in here about you. As many as I can. Help me help other guys find you like I did. Whatever time and energy I have left, that's how I want to use it—following you. I want to tell everyone what you've done and who you are.

So anything you want me to do, I'm ready.

Amen.

The man falls into a deep, dreamless sleep.

The day started like every other. Curtis got up at 5:30 a.m. He headed over to the chow lines in the central dining rooms and grabbed a pre-prepared tray with carefully proportioned food. (Minuscule variances in serving sizes between inmates can cause massive and monstrous riots.) He sat by himself at a table close to the wall. The room was filled with four-foot square wood and metal tables, all with round stools fixed to the frames on each side. Behind and above him was a vast, twelve-foot-tall, hundred-foot-wide mural that streamed panoramas of California state history from the frontier days through the Second World War.

Curtis wolfed down his food: two boiled eggs, two hash browns, two slices of wheat bread, four ounces of stewed prunes, four ounces of milk, and eight ounces of scalding-hot coffee. It was all pretty awful.

What was good, though, was being up early. Lots of guys stay in their cells and make breakfast with their electric hot pots, heating food like instant oatmeal and ramen that they purchase from the facility's commissary or "canteen." Therefore, things tend to be quiet in the mornings. Talking is never allowed during meals, of course. But the energy in the cavernous hall is just way less intense at quarter-full than when it's pushing its max, three-hundred-person capacity.

The peace and quiet was over too soon, though. The twenty-minute rule. Prisoners must eat and go in under twenty minutes.

At 7:00 a.m., Curtis went to work. Residents of North Block are required to have jobs. If an inmate messes up and loses his or just stops showing up, he's sent back into South Block. So Curtis is always careful to get over to the prison's furniture factory on time. New to the job, he spends most of his shifts hauling lumber and breathing sawdust. Every once in a while—not very often—he gets some training on the saws and lathes, which he likes. And for all of it, he makes a whopping thirty cents an hour.

At 1:00 p.m., he checked out and ate his brown-bag lunch in the upper yard, back over near North Block. Two bologna and cheese sandwiches. Two oatmeal cookies. A bag of corn nuts. All of it gone in less than five minutes. Then Curtis headed into North Block to shower and get cleaned up for his afternoon program.

New inmates are often surprised by the variety of programs available at San Quentin. As long as they're not too famous or haven't become too infamous, guys can sign up for choir, drama, poetry, or painting. They can take adult ed classes and earn their GEDs. They can participate in support groups like Alcoholics Anonymous and Narcotics Anonymous or vocational programs like carpentry, commercial cooking, even coding. They can participate in all manner of athletics—basketball, baseball, flag football, soccer, tennis. They can even sign up for yoga. There's also a running club that hosts an annual marathon inside the prison walls—105 laps around the lower yard.

The program Curtis attended earlier in the day, though, wasn't like any of those. For the past several Tuesdays, he's been attending something called Alpha. It's a program initially designed for churches to help them invite non-Christians to explore the Christian faith. It's also been adapted for jails and prisons, though, and the Protestant member of the prison's chaplaincy team has been running the program once a year inside the walls.

Curtis had actually been kind of eager to go, not that anyone could have guessed. When Reverend Foster mentioned it at chapel, the program had sounded interesting, but he played it super-cool. Internally, he's been wanting to learn more about God. Therefore, it was no big deal for him to give up one day a week of his usual afternoon pickup basketball.

But the first week of Alpha was tougher than expected. The chaplains separated the men into small groups. And according to the unspoken prison "rules," Curtis had to be either stoic or defiant— uninterested or derisive. But he *was* interested, and it was awkward and tense feeling one way but acting another. He almost didn't return the following week. But something inside him gave him the nudge he needed. And he's come back every week since.

The best part has been having guys to talk to. It hasn't been perfect, and Curtis has rarely spoken during the sessions, but his group has worked through some big questions together—meaning-of-life-type stuff. The kind of stuff he's never talked about with anyone else. The kind of stuff he's wrestled with alone at night, in his bunk, when his thoughts inevitably turned dark.

The seventh session, though, was different.

San Quentin sits on 432 windswept acres on the north side of the San Francisco Bay. Ten miles due north of the vibrant and bustling city that is the Bay's namesake. The formidable institution is California's oldest state penitentiary and one of North America's most notorious.

After the discovery of gold at Sutter's Mill in 1848, there was a massive influx of prospectors and fortune hunters and lawlessness to the San Francisco area. The city's jails soon swelled to capacity and beyond. California became a state in 1850, and the following year construction on San Quentin began. The prison opened its doors in 1852 to 68 inmates. Today, it holds about 3,750.[1] And 700 of those men are on death row, the largest condemned population in the United States.[2]

AN AERIAL VIEW OF SAN QUENTIN STATE PRISON

Called the "Arena" by inmates, San Quentin offers the most dangerous criminals of our day a brutal combination of physical confinement, grinding monotony, and the ever-present specter of ferocious violence. It's home to psychopathic serial killers and sociopathic mass murderers, and it has whole units devoted to California's beastly prison gangs: the Mexican Mafia, Nuestra Familia, the Black Guerrilla Family, the Aryan Brotherhood, and the Nazi Lowriders. Lots of angry, aggressive men packed tightly together into awful spaces.

The general population cells are all about the same: four feet wide, nine feet deep, give or take. The backs and sides are solid concrete. The fronts consist of black bars, a baker's dozen, extending from floor to ceiling and wall to wall. Inside each set of thirteen bars is a sliding, locking door.

Each cell has two stacked bunks fastened securely to the wall, a metal toilet, a metal washbasin with cold running water, and two lockers. The cells are arranged in long rows, stacked into five tiers. Poor ventilation in the cell blocks means the air is always stuffy, warm, and putrid—even when the wind is blowing fresh and cold off the water.

A 2005 court-ordered report described San Quentin as "old, antiquated, dirty, poorly staffed, poorly maintained with inadequate medical space and equipment and overcrowded."[3] The institution is currently running at about 123 percent of its designed capacity.[4]

EAST BLOCK AT SAN QUENTIN STATE PRISON

Curtis was processed into this miserable place seven years ago. He'd been in and out of county jails much of his adult life, but this is his second stint in prison. And it'll be his last, because he's never going to leave. He may get transferred to another California-based maximum-security correctional facility, for sure. That's out of his hands. But he's never getting out of the state prison system.

"Life in prison with no possibility of parole." His heart was so empty when the judge uttered those words, they didn't even bother him. Inside. Out. What did it matter?

Well, his heart isn't empty now.

Not anymore.

✦ ✦ ✦

Curtis King was born in Long Beach, Los Angeles County, in 1967. His mom and dad were young and struggled with parenthood. Less than a year after Curtis was born, his dad split. His mom worked full-time waiting tables at various restaurants and bars but struggled to hold down those jobs; she struggled with alcohol and drugs too.

Curtis spent much of his young childhood living with his mom but was also hustled around to grandparents and aunts and uncles and a couple of foster homes. His family had to find a place for him to live when his mom would disappear for long stretches. They called them her "benders." Then, around the time Curtis turned ten, for some reason, his dad sometimes let him stay over at his tiny apartment. He lived only a few miles away. So during the ensuing years, he got to see his dad with multiple girlfriends, all in whom he showed more interest than he did his own son. And that's when Curtis's bitterness began to really take hold—and turn to anger—and then to rage.

Curtis began skipping classes in high school and staying out late. No one cared. He also got into plenty of fights. At seventeen, he dropped out of high school altogether but lacked the qualifications to get a decent job. So he sold marijuana to his friends for a couple of years. Then he lied about his age and got a job as a bouncer at a local club. He'd grown tall enough and big enough to pass for someone older than nineteen.

There was violence nearly every night at the club during those years—but it all seemed normal to Curtis. The brutality was an outlet for his anger. Three times he was sentenced to stretches in LA's Men's Central Jail. Twice for assault and battery. Once for aggravated battery, because he gashed a guy's head with the bottom of a beer bottle.

Between and after those stints, Curtis continued working as a bouncer. He also worked security whenever there were concerts at The Forum in Inglewood, and he got some work as a personal bodyguard, working for a few years for some minor Hollywood celebrities. At one point, though, he got connected with the San Diego chapter of the

Hells Angels Motorcycle Club. They were selling marijuana, cocaine, PCP, and LSD—and Curtis helped with collections in the LA area. He thought nothing of putting guns to the heads of people who couldn't or wouldn't pay their debts—or just beating them senseless. "I was so coldhearted back then," he would say years later.

He got his first prison sentence for kidnapping and extortion. A Long Beach businessman owed some Hells Angels guys serious money after a mishandled drug deal. Curtis and two accomplices held the man for two days, threatening to kill him if his family didn't come up with the cash—or if they went to the police. His wife went to the police anyway, and Curtis did two years at the California Institution for Men in Chino, California.

Upon his release, Curtis went right back to his violent and lucrative ways, again working primarily with his friends out of San Diego. He managed to steer clear of the authorities for nearly five years before being arrested for capital murder. In California, capital murder is defined as "murder with special circumstances." About twenty different scenarios qualify as special circumstances. In Curtis's case, there were two: (1) murder of a witness to prevent them from testifying, and (2) murder to benefit a street gang. The penalty for capital murder is either death or life in prison without parole. Curtis got the latter. And that's how he ended up at San Quentin.

A ruthless, remorseless man.

A ruthless, remorseless, guilt-ridden man who agreed to attend a chapel service one Sunday seven years after arriving at this cruel establishment. It took only about a hundred invitations from his cellmate, who's actually a pretty decent guy, as San Quentin convicts go. A little crazy, but decent. And were it not for the fact that Curtis had gone to church a handful of times with his grandparents when his mom was drunk or high, he never would have agreed to it.

On that Sunday, though, Curtis met Reverend Chris Foster, one of the prison's hardest-working chaplains.

Rev. Foster headed to that fateful meeting through the East Gate. He entered through the main entrance, which is in the administration, or "officers and guards," building. He proceeded through two security doors, the second of which rolls open only after the first one has closed. He chatted with the receiving guard, who never fails to mention that if he's taken hostage, the warden will not negotiate for his release.

Once inside, he made his way across a courtyard to the Chapel Complex building. His office is there, and he spent a couple of hours going over his sermon and checking in with two of his colleagues. He then got down on his knees and prayed for all the inmates in the facility before walking to the chapel itself, where he got things ready for the service. He turned on the lights and arranged the chairs. He greeted men as they arrived and engaged in a few short conversations. Then, when it was time, he opened in prayer, read a Scripture passage, and launched into his short sermon.

He finished twenty minutes later, and that's when the chaplain heard Curtis's call for rescue. He heard it even beneath Curtis's tough-as-nails facade and feigned disinterest.

Calls like those are exactly why Rev. Foster does what he does. In here, they're never explicit, but every so often, an inmate will ask a question that reveals an open heart. Not too infrequently, actually, a man will ask a question that betrays a deep longing and a readiness for forgiveness. For redemption.

In Curtis's case, it began with a raised hand. The seasoned chaplain tends to be wary when hands go up because they can signal an imminent tirade of verbal abuse. Other times, though, they can be a signal that the Holy Spirit is working in a man's heart; they can be an indication not of aggression but of surrender.

"Yes, sir? In the back. Do you have a question?"

"Yeah, I do. So … what does this Jesus think about a guy like *me*?"

The men chuckled, *but that was it*. Rev. Foster knew it when he heard it.

The chaplain tossed up a quick and silent prayer. *Jesus, come. This man needs you.* He then answered Curtis with care and compassion. And that's how it started—small. Because that was Rev. Foster's style. As he'd said many times, his ministry is mostly about making himself available to inmates who want to talk. And Curtis apparently did.

The two men began meeting one on one for an hour each week, and the questions and conversation flowed. Curtis argued and got angry a few times, understandably having trouble with the idea that he could ever be forgiven. But Rev. Foster spoke of mercy and love and got him a Bible through the Gideons. He pointed Curtis toward Ezekiel: "When a wicked person turns away from the wickedness he has committed and does what is just and right, he shall save his life" (Ezek. 18:27).

The chaplain showed him the story of the penitent thief in the gospel of Luke. And the stories of Paul's conversion from a life of violence to one of peace and purpose as an apostle of Jesus. And ever so slowly, Rev. Foster could see that Curtis was letting the Holy Spirit into his heart.

Curtis still played it tough when Rev. Foster announced the Alpha course to the group. And he did again when Rev. Foster invited him personally to attend the program. The chaplain was used to being around prisoners, though, and none of Curtis's posturing bothered him. Based on their conversations, Rev. Foster knew Curtis was eager to learn more about God.

And on the first Tuesday afternoon session of Alpha, Curtis showed up and did great. He wore his hardcase mask, of course, but actually participated a little in the group discussions. And then he showed up again. And again. And then, during the seventh session, something extraordinary happened.

When one of the Alpha volunteers was wrapping up a question-and-answer time, Rev. Foster felt compelled to pray with Curtis. So as everyone was filing out of the room, he found him in the back and asked if he could.

"Sure, man. That's fine."

Come, Jesus.

The men pulled two chairs together and sat down. Rev. Foster put his hand on Curtis's head and prayed. "Father God, you love your son. Jesus, our King, you died for this man because you love him so much. Holy Spirit, come. Show Curtis right now how much you love him. Fill his heart with your presence." Then he took his hand off his head and looked Curtis right in the eye. "Now, you pray."

"About what?"

"Just let it out, brother. Pray from your heart."

"Okay." Curtis dropped his head. "Jesus, I trust you died on a cross for me. But I don't know why. I don't like who I am. Please, Jesus. Please forgive me. Help me, Jesus, to become a better man."

They sat in silence, neither man moving. Then, slowly, Curtis sensed something in his hands. Then his arms. It was a slight prickling sensation. It felt a little like fire, but it didn't hurt. Then the tears came. *They really came.* He hadn't cried since he was little. It was like twenty years of guilt and grief, sorrow and regret came rushing to the surface. He tried to hold them back by closing his eyes as tightly as he could. But it was no use.

"It's okay, Curtis. That's the Holy Spirit. That's Jesus. He just loves you, brother."

Those words broke something. It was like he was young again. He wept for five minutes at least. It was joyous, like an enormous weight lifted off his body, his heart, his life. When he finally opened his eyes again, he blinked a few times and wiped his face with the sleeve of his blue, long-sleeve, button-down California Department of Corrections and Rehabilitation shirt. He looked at Rev. Foster. It was like someone had switched on a light. He knew. He just knew. Something big had happened. Everything had changed. God was real. Jesus was in the room. That feeling in his body was the Holy Spirit.

And everything did change. It took lots of letters, but Rebekah started visiting him again. Shane too. (His boy is getting so tall.) And now Curtis performs rescues of his own. With confidence thumping in his heart, he tells hard men in the hardest of prisons about Jesus. He shares his testimony with everyone who'll listen. He even dares to tell other lifers that, while they might never be free physically, their spirits *can* be—just like his is free.

A chaplain is a religious leader employed by a secular institution rather than a church. Chaplains work in prisons and jails, hospitals, schools and universities, businesses, police and fire departments, and for military units and sports teams. The title originally referred to leaders of the Christian faith but now applies equally to leaders of all religions and philosophical traditions.

The US Department of Defense employs thousands of chaplains across the American military service branches, including the special operations forces and the Coast Guard.[5] The Navy has around eight hundred chaplains.[6] The Army, about twenty-nine hundred.[7] The American criminal justice system also employs chaplains—lots of them:

> Almost all of the nation's more than 1,100 state and federal prisons have at least one paid chaplain or religious services coordinator, and collectively they employ about 1,600 professional chaplains.[8]

The chaplaincy corps at San Quentin started slowly. An 1861 California legislative report recognized the importance of having someone to share the gospel with prisoners:

> History is replete with instances where the word of God, falling on the ear of the vilest of sinners, has conjured up some innocent memory of the past,

and by appealing to the better feelings of his nature, recalled him to a better life.[9]

The same report lamented, however, that San Quentin was woefully delinquent in this regard. "No prayer is heard," it read, "no Bible is read, no exhortation to repentance is heard."[10]

The earliest wardens, and even the prison's earliest chaplains, were more interested in providing convicts with backbreaking work and spirit-breaking discipline. "The criminal should not only be restrained of his liberty," wrote J. P. Ames, San Quentin's first professional warden, "but he should be subjected to a discipline so thorough as to prevent his again committing crimes." Ames doled out solitary confinement as a means of giving a prisoner time to "reflect upon his past career" and "to make him penitent."[11] Hence the name "penitentiary."

The work of prison chaplains today is different. The Pew Research Center published a report in 2012 based on interviews with 730 prison chaplains in all fifty states. Nearly all agreed that the following duties were their most important: leading worship services, administering religious programs, working with external faith-based and community organizations, providing religious instruction or spiritual counseling, and supervising or training volunteers.[12]

Many chaplains describe their work as ultimately providing a ministry of presence—of just being there, of companionship, of community. "When Job was cut down from family and success, his true friends came to him and just sat and listened," wrote Rev. Earl Smith, chaplain at San Quentin for many years. "A good chaplain," he wrote, "has to learn to be an excellent listener."[13]

Chaplains at large federal and state facilities also work in teams, cooperating and supporting one another just like the members of search-and-rescue outfits and hotshot crews do. "The size of the chaplaincy team is generally determined by the number of inmates in the population and the complexity of the institution mission," said Rev. Carlos Gonzales, who works for the Federal Bureau of Prisons. "The word *team* is key," he said, "in that all Bureau of Prisons chaplains, regardless of their own faith orientation, are expected to minister as an effective pastoral team to an entire inmate population."[14]

And these hardworking, heroic men and women do it for one reason: to see people rescued. Writing about his time in the Arena, Rev. Smith wrote this:

I loved the men and seeing their lives changed. I loved seeing families made whole again. I loved seeing barriers broken and reconciliation and healing take place. Where else in ministry can you see God's transforming power at work in such a significant manner on a daily basis? Each day I went to work, I expected to be part of a miracle. I expected God to do something special.[15]

SAN FRANCISCO BAY

NORTH BLOCK

SAN QUENTIN STATE PRISON

CHAPEL COMPLEX

HOLY BIBLE

San Quentin State Prison
Northern California

Opened: July 1852 to 68 inmates
Current Prison Population: 3,750 Inmates
Current Prison Ministry Team: 5 Chaplains

S
E W
N

BELiEF:
CHRISTIAN COMMUNITY
IS NOT COOL.

Do you ever think, *People are always saying that Christians should be in community. But I'm sorry, it's just not for me. It's dull and awkward and, frankly, a waste of time. I'm sure some people find those groups helpful, but I just don't get anything out of sitting in uncomfortable chairs, drinking stale coffee, giving obvious answers to canned questions.*

This kind of thinking is rooted neither in truth nor in the goodness of God. *Think again.*

Followers of Jesus, wrote A. W. Tozer, "ought to be the most fearless, most relaxed, most utterly self-assured—or God-assured—people of the wide world and the happiest people."[16] He was right. No matter the circumstances we find ourselves in, we ought to be confident because we are sons of the God of the Universe. We are beloved sons of God Almighty, clothed in his favor, filled with his Spirit, and led by the conqueror who broke us out of sin's prison. The legendary one who defeated even death.

We ought to walk and work, wherever we go, not in fear but with a mystical, everlasting confidence, just like Lieutenant Cummings did. Not ever in arrogance but in the secure knowledge that we are forgiven, free, and in our weakness made stronger than we can fully comprehend. We ought to walk and work with confidence not because we think we're better than anyone else but because we've humbled ourselves and let ourselves be rescued. Because we've stopped pushing God and our brothers away and because we let them rescue us over and over.

We ought to walk and work with confidence because we are fully loved, fully forgiven members of Spirit-filled rescue teams—men's groups that accept us and have our backs no matter what.

How do we get there? That *is* the question. And now it's time to answer it.

Nothing is more important.

We men like things to be concrete. We tend to like answers more than questions. And we love it when someone just gives us those answers. We like gear lists and checklists. And we tend to believe that, if equipped with the right answers, things will go well. Just tell us what's good and bad, right and wrong, and we'll go crush it.

In our spiritual lives, we often assume that growth occurs (or doesn't) and that community builds and thrives (or doesn't) mostly because we've checked all the right boxes (or failed to). We have a strong inclination, therefore, to follow the approaches and practices of other men. We're inclined to draft behind pastors, leaders, or anyone else who appears to have things all figured out. But here's the truth: while loving God and loving other people *is* the formula for building and maintaining authentic Christian community, exactly how we apply that formula to our complicated lives and complex situations is never so simple. There are no universally applicable bullet points we can slap into a PDF and pass around among ourselves.

But there *is* a guide. There's an energizing and inspiring, present and available Spirit. Jesus promised that "he will guide [us] into all the truth" (John 16:13). Rest assured, therefore, the Holy Spirit *will* whisper into your heart and invite you into community. He *will* guide you as you build community. And he *will* help you and your brothers maintain it, as long as the particular group is the right one for you.

What will it look like? I don't know. All of God's rescue teams are different. You're unique. Your crew is unique. God's family is wonderfully diverse. The Holy Spirit will deal with each of us differently. You should feel free, therefore, to follow him and do your own thing. But trust me, you *will* find something that works for you.

Scripture and common sense provide helpful and trustworthy guardrails, of course. But groups can vary how they express these principles and values based on preferences and contexts. Different groups can employ different practices with different intensities. And they should.

Therefore, I encourage you to refrain from imitating what anyone else is doing or has done. Just because structures and approaches have worked for someone else doesn't mean they'll work for you. They might. But don't assume it. Many groups falter and fail because they end up talking about the wrong stuff and engaging in the wrong practices, which would leave anyone feeling frustrated and disconnected and looking for the exit. But it doesn't have to be like that.

We should applaud others. We should cheer them on. We should allow their stories to be invitations and inspiration for us. But we must cut our own paths, following the same Spirit. This sentiment was captured by a group of Quakers, people who, in seventeenth-century England, decided to root their lives in direct and distinctive experiences of God:

> We do not want you to copy or imitate us. We want to be like a ship that has crossed the ocean, leaving a wake of foam, which soon fades away. We want you to follow the Spirit, which we have sought to follow, but which must be sought anew in every generation.[17]

As you think about *your* rescue team—*the one that fits you*—here are some things to think about. Here are some ideas to kick around as you get started. What you do with each of these, though, is entirely up to you.

PERMISSION

One of the first things I did when forming the Table group was to meet with the man who led my former group, the Cave. I went to see him at his office to ask for advice. "I'm going to tell you everything I know about starting and leading a company of men," he said. I was eager to hear what he was going to say. I remember being hunched over a yellow legal pad, clutching a ballpoint pen, in position to write furiously. I didn't want to miss a thing.

"Are you ready?"

"I am."

"Okay. Here's everything I know: Start every meeting with a prayer of invitation. Give the Spirit permission to work. Invite him to be your guide."

I wrote it down and waited enthusiastically for the next piece of wisdom.

"That's it," he said. "If you pray a prayer of invitation before every meeting—and if you mean what you pray—you'll do great."

My friends and I followed his instructions. And looking back, years later, I can see it. He was right. The input and influence of the Holy Spirit are what made all the difference. They are what brought us together and kept us together. They made transformation and healing and rescue possible. Trappist monk and priest Basil Pennington wrote, "Ordinary people can live in the victory of community, though not by their own doing; it is possible only through God's working in and among them."[18] He was right too.

The input and influence of the Holy Spirit were available to the earliest followers of Jesus. They've been available to every Christian since. And they're available to us. We just have to ask. But the asking is important. We don't have to ask for his presence. He'll be there already, for sure. He won't force his input and influence, though. We need to give him permission to bring those things into our groups, our lives, and our hearts.

COMMITMENT

No one is ever forced to join a search-and-rescue outfit, a hotshot crew, or a chaplaincy team in a prison. But once someone does, he or she is expected to adopt an *all-in, all-the-time* attitude.

No one is forced to join a spiritual rescue team either. But if we do, we should be ready to adopt a similar mindset. We should be ready to fight, day in and day out, shoulder to shoulder with our brothers, to fight the big battles and face the daily struggles together too. We should be ready to show up faithfully. Prepared to engage and contribute. Prepared to be there for our brothers when they need us.

"Love one another with brotherly affection," wrote the apostle Paul (Rom. 12:10). Rescue teams run on this kind of love, and the more of it there is, the better they run. In fact, the degree to which communities of men thrive is directly correlated to the degree to which those men are willing to commit their time and energy to one another. The more anyone puts in, the more everyone gets out.

COVENANT

Many men's groups discuss expectations and boundaries explicitly and up front. Some even write things down. For others, expectations and boundaries are simply implied. All groups, though, rely on some sort of mutual agreement—for example, about where to meet, how long to meet, what will be discussed, who will lead, what the overall goals are for the group. Most groups will also come to an understanding on confidentiality and accountability.

These kinds of agreements, whether explicit or implicit, are essentially promises we make to one another, and they govern life together. We sometimes refer to them as *covenants*, named just like the promises God makes to his sons and daughters.

Covenants explicitly discussed can spur us to take our commitments more seriously than we might otherwise. And perhaps most importantly, they can facilitate the creation of safe places characterized by trust. For example, covenants that spell out expectations about confidentiality can result in groups in which men are more apt to be honest, because members are perhaps more likely to trust that things said in the group will be treated with care and held in strict confidence.

It's important to point out, though, that covenants are human creations. We can never trust them completely because they are compromised by human frailty. Even the closest of friends are human and capable of unkindness and even betrayal, whether we have covenants in place or not. Our confidence, therefore, should be first and foremost in our God, who will never let us down.

God will empower our commitments to our brothers and theirs to us. He will help us be faithful to one another. And when he calls us to be honest and vulnerable with our brothers, we can trust him, even when it might not go so well. It usually does, but sometimes it might not (at least from our perspective). Even that's okay. It'll go well from God's perspective; our obedience to him always does. He knows better than we do.

And when we blow it, when a brother hurts or betrays us—or we, them—he'll help us forgive each other and heal and, hopefully, restore those relationships to something even more substantial.

ONBOARDING

When a new man joins a rescue team, it's often helpful for existing members to discuss the group's history—why it formed and what God's done there. It's good to discuss beliefs, values, practices, traditions, and the meanings behind them all. It's good to discuss goals and expectations too. We all need to know what we're signing up for: what will be required of us and what we can count on from our brothers.

Trial periods can also be beneficial. Joining a group is a big decision, and men should have time to gather information, pray, and discern whether a group is right for them and whether they're ready to accept the cost of a commitment and a covenant.

It is also kind to offer a graceful exit if a man decides against joining.

SIZE AND STANCE

Minimums are easy. One man isn't a group; two is. Beyond that, things get murky because there is no universally optimal size for these groups. It depends on the men and the circumstances and the season. Larger groups, more than four or five perhaps, tend to be more dynamic, more lively, and more stable. But men can feel lost or forgotten in larger groups. In smaller groups, it's easier to create an atmosphere of trust. It's also easier for men to have a chance to talk week to week, to check in, to be known.

Ultimately, it's for God to decide and us to discern who and how many brothers should be in our rescue teams. It's for him to decide whether our groups should be open or closed, whether they should expand beyond the initial members or not, or beyond specific numbers of men.

The Table, the group I helped run for ten years, was open. The leaders and I trusted that that was God's will. As such, we stopped trying to figure out whether any new man was supposed to become a member or not. We welcomed everyone but also prayed every so often that God send us the right men. We prayed that certain men would hear and respond to God's whispers in their hearts—whispers to come, to join. That stance freed us from having to worry about optimal group size. God was in charge of membership.

Not all groups, though, should be open. For example, ones that find themselves in seasons of significant conflict should probably not be welcoming new members. If we are at odds, our focus should be on reconciliation, not on inviting others into our dysfunction.

The same goes for groups that are brand new. New groups generally need time to coalesce. Men need time to get to know one another. The same goes for groups that have reached capacity. Groups may need to close for a season because they've simply gotten too large.

If you sense from God that you should refuse a man for any of these or any other reasons, you should not feel guilty. Award-winning author Edith Schaeffer wrote, "Because there are more people than we have time or strength to see personally and care for, it is imperative to remember that it is not sinful to be finite and limited."[19]

But we should never refuse a man out of fear—for example, fear of how the group might change. We should only refuse a man when we sense that it's God's will. Otherwise, we should do everything we can to welcome him. We should take risks and have the courage to accommodate as many as we can. But if we do discern that refusal is the right course, we must be honest and kind and offer alternatives. To be turned away is nearly always a wounding experience.

We should also not feel bad when a man decides not to join our group. That's up to him—and God. Our job is to love, not to save. And we should never override the man's discernment (or anyone else's) and try to force community. We should never impose our will on any other man. We must follow God's lead and respect our brothers' choices.

In terms of stance, what's ultimately most important is that we are open to God. We may or may not be open to new members, but we should always be open to him. If he wants our group to be open and we discern that, then great; we should be open. If he wants our group to be closed for a season, then great; we should listen and do that instead.

As I write this, I am now part of a rescue team that split off from the Table. It's new and small. But we are open to God's leading. We don't always hear his voice and sense his will perfectly, but we make every effort to listen. We pray a lot and make the best decisions we can based on what we sense and discern. We recently grew from two men to six.

FUNCTION AND FOCUS

Because we are physical beings, we need physical proximity to forge relationships with our brothers, even if that sometimes means digital proximity. *Face to face* may have come to mean something different in recent years, as so many of us experienced during the COVID-19 pandemic. But it's still nonnegotiable. We can experience community over

Zoom (if we have to), but we cannot find it on Netflix or YouTube. For community to happen, there must be at least one other living, breathing person immediately involved, somehow.

Both Scripture and tradition offer another nonnegotiable: to be in authentic Christian community, we should be doing some suitable combination of studying Scripture, worshipping, engaging in conversation, confessing to one another, keeping each other accountable, encouraging each other, serving one another, praying with and for each other, and celebrating together.

But even for rescue teams that do most or all of these things, the details can be quite different. For example, some groups thrive by being study-focused, approaching God from a more intellectual perspective. Some groups thrive by being more Bible-focused, coming to God by reading and discussing Scripture. Some groups thrive as book groups. Some groups thrive by focusing more on updates and sharing what's going on in their lives. Some groups thrive as accountability groups, especially ones that form among men struggling with a particular issue or addiction. Some groups come together around prayer. Some groups thrive by sharing specific aspects of their lives like meals or a particular form of exercise.

Again, individual discernment is crucial.

FREQUENCY AND DURATION

Modern men are busy. It can be tempting to consider meeting every other week or even once a month. Many groups do. In my experience, though, rescue teams need to meet at least once a week if at all possible.

To be a rescue team, we need to be *in* our brothers' lives, and they need to be in ours. We need to be checking in with one another. We need to know the mundane details of each other's days. We need to be involved in both the daily battles and the overwhelming struggles, and everything in between. But it's difficult to be that involved if we're meeting less frequently than weekly. It can also be difficult to build and maintain group momentum when we meet less often. If we let too much time elapse between meetings, we lose continuity, and it can feel like each time we are beginning anew.

There is also the issue of absences. When a group meets every other week, for example, and one of the members misses a meeting, it'll be a full month between meetings for him. That's a very long time to be disconnected.

In terms of meeting duration, I believe two hours is a minimum, and that's for smaller groups. Relationships don't form and thrive when hurried. We need time to talk. We need to let conversations run their courses. We need room to think about and respond to issues and questions as they arise—and time to return to things if necessary. We also need to give the Holy Spirit the time he needs to work in our hearts. He doesn't work on our schedules. In my experience, it's better to allow a full three hours. Running longer than that, though, can cause men to tire and struggle to maintain attention.

LEADERSHIP

Authentic Christian communities are inclusive and tend to be flat in terms of their power structures. Everyone brings something valuable and unique. By the power of the Holy Spirit, everyone is capable of contributing in their own God-given ways. Our spiritual giftings vary. We have different talents and personalities and experiences. For rescue teams to function as intended, we must recognize and appreciate one another, including these differences.

Having said that, groups usually need leaders. One of the spiritual gifts* is, indeed, the gift of leadership (see Rom. 12:3–8). The Spirit supercharges some people to lead the rest of us. And that's a good thing, because leaderless groups can be challenging. Even with just a few members, groups that try to share leadership can lose energy and

---

* For a listing of spiritual gifts, please see appendix A of the first book in the WiRE Series for Men, *Invention: Break Free from the Culture Hell-Bent on Holding You Back.*

focus. In our busy world, groups typically need a torchbearer. Someone to watch and listen and guide.

As groups mature, though, it usually becomes easier and more appropriate to share leadership more broadly. Over time, men grow into spiritual giftings and develop leadership capabilities. But in the beginning, groups typically need an instigator. That is, in fact, how most rescue teams get started: someone senses a fire in their heart and takes action.

If two or three men feel called to lead together, that can work well. It can bring vitality and stability. Each leader will bring his own ideas and gifts. Multiple leaders can also share the burden, reducing the likelihood of burnout. They can cover for each other when someone is traveling or unavailable on a given day. They can also provide each other accountability and prayer support.

Whatever leadership looks like, it should be rooted in a call to serve. Our spiritual gifts are given to us *for the benefit of others*, and our callings to put those gifts to work should come from God. A calling might come *through* other men, for example, when a group trusts someone among their ranks and asks him to lead. But even then, the call must be confirmed by the man himself; he should not accept out of ambition or obligation or guilt.

It's also important to be careful with our expectations of leaders. We must let them lead in their own ways, in their particular giftings, and not force them to fit our preconceived notions. We mustn't undercut their leadership because they're not doing it the way we would or the way someone else has done it in the past.

We should also make sure to support our leaders even when they bring disruption. If a man is walking with God, trying to hear his voice, he'll often be an unsettling force to those around him, encouraging the rest of the group to get out of their comfort zones, into confession, into healing. And even though disruption can be annoying and we tend to resist it, we should be grateful and respectful toward leaders who are doing their best to follow Jesus.

It is also good, though, to establish limits on power. No matter who a leader is, no matter how accomplished or impressive, the men in the group should feel empowered to speak up and push back, if necessary and appropriate. All leaders mess up. It will happen. And when it does, mistakes and tensions should be handled according to Scripture:

> If your brother sins against you, go and tell him his fault, between you and him alone. If he listens to you, you have gained your brother. But if he does not listen, take one or two others along with you, that every charge may be established by the evidence of two or three witnesses. If he refuses to listen to them, tell it to the church. And if he refuses to listen even to the church, let him be to you as a Gentile and a tax collector. (Matt. 18:15–17)

When a leader makes a mistake, we should try to be understanding. We should be forgiving without losing confidence, unless of course, he's unrepentant, the missteps are chronic, and the resulting tensions jeopardize the existence of the group. In those rare circumstances, the group should pray together and discuss and discern whether to remove a leader. And if the decision is made to remove him, even that should be done with love and care. Remember how Jesus treated Gentiles and tax collectors.

It can be challenging to be aware of everything that's going on in a room. It's easy for any leader to miss the nonverbal cues emanating from men who are hurting but reluctant to speak up. It's easy for leaders to miss the promptings and movements of the Holy Spirit too. For example, instead of continuing with an agenda, the members of a group might need to pause whatever they're doing, turn their attention to a particular man, and pray together.

Therefore, it can be beneficial to empower a man who is *not* leading and put him in a watchman's role. He can be alert and mindful of the room's mood and the apparent state of men's hearts when the leader cannot. He can be quietly prayerful with full permission to interrupt whatever is going on when he sees or senses a need.

DECISIONS AND CONFLICTS

When a group begins experiencing authentic community, the way it makes decisions and resolves conflicts will shift. How it does this, wrote Scott Peck, is "something inherently almost mystical, magical."[20] Groups will tend to move beyond hierarchy, beyond democracy even. "Decisions in genuine community," wrote Peck, "are arrived at through consensus."[21]

Leaders still lead, but everyone has a voice. Everyone's voice is valued and included, even when they differ. Because of the presence of God's Spirit in our hearts and because of the personal healing and spiritual growth that have already occurred, consensus is possible. "Where God is at work things suddenly succeed which otherwise constantly fail," wrote the German priest and theologian Gerhard Lohfink.[22]

This is not to say that things will always go well. They won't. Rescue teams are rostered with real people who are in real relationships with one another. Meetings will go poorly. Tensions will rise. But again, because of the presence of the Holy Spirit and the work he's doing in our hearts, conflict can begin to be a positive thing. It can force issues into the open and us into prayer. Conflicts and tensions can push us apart, of course, but they can also bring us back together even more closely. We get to know one another (and God) when we share difficult circumstances. We can become deeper friends.

RULES

In my experience, men's groups benefit from having some simple rules in place, but not so many that men feel stifled or controlled. And those rules should always be about one thing: love. For Christians, this is really the only rule.

Here's a sampling of a few simple rules that have worked in my groups:

We talk mostly about ourselves.

It's easier to talk about other people. It's easier to deflect and talk instead about kids or wives or friends rather than opening up. To honestly share our lives, though, we must share what is going on in *our* hearts. I encourage men, therefore, to talk mostly about themselves, to relate their own stories. When they talk about other people, I encourage them to talk about them only from their own perspectives.

When we approach the topic of sin, this rule becomes even more critical simply because of how much we dislike talking about our own. It's easier to blame or point out how others have failed than to confess our own failures. But we don't grow and mature by pointing at others. We get better by taking responsibility for our contributions to problems and disputes.

Therefore, I encourage men to confess only their own sin and never that of others. Talking about struggles with other people is okay to provide context. But I steer men away from gossiping, scrutinizing, blaming, or judging anyone else, especially when those people aren't in the room to defend themselves (like spouses).

We don't talk behind each other's backs.

When another group member has hurt or frustrated or annoyed us, it's natural to want to engage a close friend or two in an offline conversation about it. If such discussions are focused on sharing our hearts or seeking wisdom, that's one thing. If it turns into criticizing or ranting or gossiping about the source of our discontent, that will only hurt community.

God does not give us brothers to accuse them but that we might forgive. This does not mean that we are to avoid tough conversations. To pretend a hurt doesn't exist, to push it down and leave it unaddressed, is also quite harmful to relationships. We must address tensions directly and honestly and in ways that are loving and preserving of our brothers' dignity.

We don't assign homework.
Whenever I've tried using books or studies that require weekly reading, I've found it challenging to keep everyone on the same schedule without undue pressure. Despite the best of intentions, many men today will struggle to keep up with reading assignments. This makes group discussions awkward. It also increases the risk that men will drop off, because no one wants to show up chronically unprepared. I have, therefore, at times instituted a no-homework policy.

This rule doesn't work for all groups, of course. Some groups succeed precisely because their members have the capacity and the desire for outside study. I encourage you to pray and make a realistic and honest assessment of your fellow members' interests and obligations.

STORIES

One of the first things a man should offer to any group is his story. It's usually too much to ask a man on his first or second meeting to give more than an easy three- to five-minute *Who are you and why are you here?* story. By the time a man decides to join a group, though, he should be ready and willing to offer as much of his story as he can manage, and we should give him plenty of time to do so. I find that a man will typically need an hour.

Rescue teams cannot operate if we don't know one another, and we get to know one another first by telling our stories. If we never hear them, we're likely to wound each other and damage community, for example, by giving advice and trying to "fix" a person or a situation that we don't fully understand. We need to know a man's background and struggles to become his brother. To be able to speak the truth to him, in love.

When it comes time for a man to tell his story, I encourage him to be as honest and vulnerable as possible and to start at the beginning. And I encourage everyone gathered to give him their full attention but refrain from interrupting with questions.

I ask that everyone also refrain from yawning, whispering, checking phones, looking at watches, or anything dishonoring like that.

The exercise is hard enough without such things. We're used to talking about successes and joys, but talking about mistakes and hardship is difficult. We want to give men a safe place and all the time they need. If a man resists, I don't push. I don't pressure. I'll meet with him one on one and try to figure out the source of the resistance. Then, at some point, I'll invite him again, gently.

And when a man finishes, I thank him for honoring the group by trusting us with his honesty and vulnerability. I welcome a few questions but caution the men gathered to keep them encouraging and open-ended, not meant to reject or debunk anything that was said. We can offer our kind curiosity and perhaps prompt him to go a bit deeper. But if there's any resistance, again, I back off. It's good to encourage more profound vulnerability, but we never want to force it.

Lastly, because men often join rescue teams at different times, it can be challenging to make sure all of the men in a group have heard everyone else's stories. This is especially true when groups get larger. Therefore, new men are typically at a disadvantage, having offered their own without having heard many or any other stories. It can make sense, then, to cycle back through everyone's stories every so often—perhaps making time for the exercise once a year.

VULNERABILITY AND CONFESSION

Men in rescue teams should never stop telling their stories. As we add new chapters, we must keep our brothers current. We must keep one another updated about new experiences, new circumstances, new struggles, new failures, new fears, new successes, as well as new insights about past experiences. And we must be willing to confess new sins.

Confession is critical because a pattern of rescue will emerge in the lives of men who engage in it regularly. The pattern goes like this: sin, confession, repentance, small change; sin, confession, repentance, small change; and so on. When it's a part of our lives, this pattern ensures that we grow and get better over time—that sins change and lessen in severity as the cycles progress. Its presence makes it less likely that we get stuck too deeply in our sin ever again.

Where the pattern typically breaks down, though, is in the confession phase. No man likes that part. In our culture of pretended perfection, pretended invulnerability, it's humiliating to let anyone see our frailty. "It hurts," wrote Bonhoeffer, "it cuts a man down, it is a dreadful blow to pride."[23] So most of us try to avoid confession at all costs, and we try to battle sin on our own.

But no matter how hard, or how many times, we fight, that approach won't work. When we go it alone, we remain trapped. And we can remain trapped for years—*for decades*—too afraid to call out for help and prayer for fear of what our brothers will think of us.

That's why rescue teams must be *safe* places. In such places, in authentic community, wrote Bonhoeffer, a man "can dare to be a sinner."[24] A man can dare to humble himself in front of his brothers because he trusts they will be merciful. In rescue teams, we acknowledge that *all* of us are sinners, not just the man confessing—and that makes it easier for everyone to come clean. Men feel less alone and will begin revealing their brokenness because they trust that, when they do, they'll still be loved and accepted and valued.

> "If a Christian is in the fellowship of confession
> with a brother he will never be alone again,
> anywhere."[25] —Dietrich Bonhoeffer

The men of the Cave shocked me with the boldness of their vulnerability. They were courageous in their confessions and created an environment where I was willing to talk about my struggles with sin for the first time in my life. It wasn't easy, but it changed my life. And those early confessions have become some of my proudest moments.

When we confess to our brothers, they can pray for us. They can speak the truth in love. We can repent. And they can also stand in place of Jesus and forgive. For we have, as Bonhoeffer wrote, "the authority to hear the confession of sin and to forgive sin in his name."[26] And then we can change. And *that's* the cycle. Whenever and wherever it exists, many men will be saved.

ACCOUNTABILITY

Without community, it's difficult, perhaps impossible, to grow and mature into the men we're meant to be. The route is winding. There are lots of twists and turns. It's a process of getting off track and getting back on—again and again. And we need help with that. We must tell our stories and confess on an ongoing basis, but we must also empower our brothers to help us find the path again whenever we've wandered off.

We must give them permission to speak to us "the truth in love" (Eph. 4:15). Speaking that way requires going beyond being polite to one another. It requires lots of kindness, but it's never kind to shy away from tough conversations. It's never kind to ignore or excuse sin or be complacent about something that is harmful to another person.

That said, speaking truth in love isn't simply about pointing out sin or shortcomings or what bothers us or what we think might bother God. It isn't about calling each other *out*. No, it's about calling each other *in*—into true identity. And it sometimes requires us to call each other away from sin ("You don't need to do that anymore ...") and into the identities God had in mind when he made us ("... because this is who you *really* are").

It starts with an appropriate level of interest in each other's flourishing, in both our lives and our relationships with God. But *interest* doesn't mean pressuring or forcing specific actions or beliefs. It means helping each other, if we want help, to heal from past wounds and to overcome mistaken beliefs. It means helping each other, if we want help, to grow in self-awareness and to become more fully ourselves. It means listening for God's voice together and on each other's behalf and discerning how God is moving in our lives and working in our hearts.

What this actually looks like will depend on the people and the circumstances, of course. Larry Crabb explained it this way:

It may be a rebuke, a piece of homey advice, even a joke that occurs to them. It may be a thought from Scripture or a memory from their past they want to share. It's rarely clever, it rarely generates admiration of the messenger's brilliance, though it may create a longing to be similarly sensitive to God's Spirit. Whatever it is, whether a hard word or a warm hug, it comes from heaven to us through a member of Christ's body. And we *know* it.[27]

And all of this is so that we can "grow up healthy in God, robust in love" (Eph. 4:16).[28]

IDENTITY

Our culture has lots to say about the men we should become. But we need to discover who God *made us* to become, and Christian community can be well-suited to that task: guiding one another into identity and truth. As brothers, we are uniquely positioned to "encourage one another and build one another up" (1 Thess. 5:11). We can look for what's right and good in each other and do our "best to bring it out" (1 Thess. 5:15).[29]

Our brothers, knowing us like few others do, can see what we don't. They can see what's true and what's false when we have a hard time distinguishing. They can see through the confusion and beyond wounds. They can see a bit of what God sees and to convey it with authority and credibility. When they tell us something, because they know us, we tend to believe it. True, God-given identities, therefore, can take hold in God-led communities in ways that they don't elsewhere.*

---

* To learn how to discover your God-given identity, please see the first book in the WiRE Series for Men, *Invention: Break Free from the Culture Hell-Bent on Holding You Back.*

At the Table, we had a heavy focus on identity. In some seasons, we spent as much as a quarter to a third of our time working to help each other discover our true identities. And whenever we believed we'd found something out about ourselves, we encouraged one another into a *bold move*—into an action or series of actions that aligned with what we'd discovered. I've made some of the weightiest decisions and undertaken some of the most important projects of my life based on those encouragements from my brothers.

Our heavy focus on identity also deepened and enriched our brotherhood. It always does, because when men begin to discover and operate in their true, God-given identities, group interactions become even more powerful. That's when rescue teams become elite. The more that men move into true identity, the more God can operate through them, and the more the group will move in love and rescue.

PRAYER

Prayer is mighty. It allows us to call the most powerful force in the universe into any situation. It enables us to call for God's unending love and immeasurable grace right into any circumstance or question or problem, even the most intractable. God may not, of course, answer in ways we want or expect. But he will answer. "Ask, and it will be given to you; seek, and you will find; knock, and it will be opened to you" (Matt. 7:7). And his answer will be the right one every time, supported by his perfect love.

Praying is, therefore, the most important thing we can do for each other. It should be central to our gatherings as rescue teams. We should be praying *with* our brothers when we are with them; we should be praying *for* them when we are not.

When we meet, it's also important to be willing to stop and pray in the moment whenever someone feels an inclination to pray for a man or a situation, even when meetings are in full swing, even when our conversations are lively. Those urges are often the Holy Spirit's promptings, and we mustn't ignore them or delay. During a meeting, it can be tempting to wait until the end to pray, or until the following week. But when a moment passes, we often get distracted and forget. So we shouldn't push aside these opportunities because we've got a schedule. God knows what he's doing.

LISTENING PRAYER

We must not forget that while we gather into rescue teams to be together and do life with our brothers, we gather to be with God first and foremost. It's imperative, therefore, that we involve him as much as we can. We should be listening for his voice and trying to discern his will as much as possible, and that means being quiet.

In the men's groups I've been a part of, we engaged in listening prayer regularly. We would ask questions—open-ended or specific—and sit together in silence, maybe for five minutes, maybe longer. Then we would discuss what we sensed or heard, what came to mind while we prayed. Some men wouldn't sense anything, and that was perfectly fine. But some men would. And we would invariably be astonished by the truth and power and wisdom that resulted from those times of listening.

WORSHIP

For many years, I struggled with worship. It was the part of a church service when my mind was most apt to wander. Sometimes I sang quietly. Sometimes I just mouthed the words. Once or twice, I think I might have hummed. But then some friends taught me how to truly worship.

I was at a retreat in the Rocky Mountains. There were maybe forty of us hanging out in the main room of a lodge. One guy was playing a guitar, while another strummed a mandolin and a third banged on some drums—and it was loud. Most of us stood, and for the first time, I worshipped God with my whole heart. Something opened in my soul. It was the first time I had sung to God at the top of my lungs. It was marvelous.

After that experience, worship became normal for me. In fact, it became, for me, another one of those nonnegotiables. I need to worship and not only in the mountains with a sold-out-for-God bluegrass band. I need to worship with my Spotify playlists in the mornings. I need to worship with my brothers when we meet. I need good worship music playing in my earbuds while I work. That day in Colorado, I realized that I was *made* to worship. You are too. Worship is, as A. W. Tozer wrote, "something built into human nature."[30]

But why should we worship in community? Well, when we gather, it works to disconnect us from the darkness of the world—from selfishness, discontent, envy, complaint. And it aligns us with truth. It prepares our hearts and minds to be together. As we worship, we become more alive to the Spirit and more likely to notice what God's doing in our midst. We also become more likely to be present for our brothers and more able to reflect God's love.

The tricky part for men is, of course, figuring out *how* to worship. "Different fellowships will require different forms of worship," wrote Bonhoeffer. "This is as it should be."[31] Like so much about community, there is no right or wrong way to do it. It's a personal choice because our relationships with God are unique. We just need to discover for ourselves what kinds of things work to shift our attention from the brokenness of the world to the goodness of God—and there are lots of possibilities.

Live music works if someone in the group is a musician. Recorded music works. Simply talking can work too. I've sometimes encouraged men to spend a few minutes telling short stories of blessing and gratitude, stories of how God has been working in their lives. I've also urged men to worship in silence. A few times, we set aside a few minutes at the very beginning of a meeting to tell God who he is for us. Each one of us, in the silence, spoke in our minds the truth of his character, or recounted how he'd come through for us in the past.

CELEBRATION

One of my favorite spiritual disciplines is celebration. Besides our families, no one is better positioned to celebrate with us than our brothers. They know us. They know our wounds and how we've blown it, and they love us still—and we love them too. Honestly and earnestly, they can celebrate our victories and joys. And together, we can celebrate what God has done for us, what he is doing, and what we know he will do in the future. We can celebrate being together—that we are no longer alone in this world. In that kind of freedom, genuine laughter and merriment often just burst forth.

And when they do, we experience a bit of heaven, which we need. Since we're more than just physical beings, it's imperative that we sometimes put our troubles and worries aside for a few hours and experience and enjoy the kinds of high spirits and good humor that are unobtainable outside the manifest presence of God.

Music and laughter, food and drink remind us that, someday soon, everything's going to be okay. They help us to revel in the truth that God's light is infinitely more powerful than any darkness. That his love is more powerful than sickness and hatred and war. That his life, the life that dwells inside each of us, is more powerful than sin and death.

SURRENDER

There's no perfect group. Outside of God himself, perfection is an illusion and a distraction. Imperfect people doing life together is never going to go perfectly. If we want every interaction, every meeting to be a mountaintop experience, we'll be disappointed. We will experience moments of near perfection, of course—times of beauty and laughter and connection and healing. But there will be mundane and messy moments too. Lots of those. Authentic community is characterized as much by difficulty and sacrifice as it is by joy and wonder.

Tensions and meetings that go badly are to be expected. And they are actually essential. So much of the goodness of community is unseen;

it flows into our hearts and our lives just by being together. We grow in times of shared trials. We bond in times of boredom. This doesn't mean we should ignore tensions, wallow in boredom, or disregard mistakes. We shouldn't. It just means we shouldn't fall into dissatisfaction or flee, expecting some ideal that we will never realize.

Also, community takes time to develop. So instead of assessing how things are going after just one or two meetings, it can be helpful to look at things over more extended periods. It's easier to gain perspective on how we're growing or how relationships are becoming more profound and more beautiful over periods of months or years than it is after only days or weeks together—especially when any of the meetings in those shorter intervals have gone badly.

FORGIVENESS

When Peter asked Jesus how many times he must forgive a brother who sins against him, he ventured a guess: "As many as seven times?" Peter asked. No, said Jesus, "I do not say to you seven times, but seventy-seven times" (Matt. 18:21–22).

Men blow it. Men doing their level best to follow Jesus blow it a lot. We should, therefore, expect lots of mistakes and missteps by us and by our brothers. We should expect imperfection—*and we should be forgiving.*

Within our rescue teams, we should create cultures of forgiveness. In the face of slights, unkind words, and careless acts, we should try to assume the deep-down goodness of our brothers. We should try to see things from larger perspectives, for example, by remembering that they, too, are living in a dark world and are very likely doing the best they can. By remembering that our brothers are wounded and by acknowledging the pain they're experiencing. And by recognizing that we aren't perfect either.

It can be exceedingly tricky, of course, to forgive someone who has really hurt us. But God will help. If we trust and follow him, he will help us do what we never thought we could. "What is impossible with man is possible with God" (Luke 18:27).

SEPARATION

Being part of a rescue team means hanging in there with our brothers even when things get tough. That said, there are times when separation is appropriate.

For example, if a man is determined to leave, that's his choice, even if we might disagree. "Our brother's ways are not in our hands; we cannot hold together what is breaking," wrote Bonhoeffer.[32] A man might decide a group has become stifling or that he has outgrown it— or maybe he feels called to break off and start another group. Painful as those decisions might be, we must respect them. And in nearly all cases, the decision to split off and create another group should be encouraged, supported, and celebrated.

It can also, however, become appropriate to ask a man to leave. Rescue teams have limits and limitations. They cannot abide nor solve every problem. Ignoring or excusing severe issues is not healthy. Trying to solve problems beyond the capabilities of a group is arrogant and likely to cause additional issues.

Sometimes a man begins struggling with something that he refuses to recognize, deal with, and heal from. Sometimes a man decides he's no longer willing to live within the covenant of a group. Or a man can become disruptive to the group's essential goals. Or someone can start causing dissension through deceit or manipulation. In such cases, separation should be considered, but only as a last resort. And it should never be effected without considerable discussion and mature discernment.

There are also times when entire fellowships have run their course and should disband. This is not necessarily a bad thing. "The longevity of a community is no more adequate a measure of its success than the length of an individual human life," wrote Scott Peck.[33] We must be open to God's leading, even when he calls us to painful things. Perhaps a group is no longer in a place of growth. Maybe it's lost its focus or its edge. Perhaps its season has passed. Or maybe it's been a place of so much growth that it's now time to break it apart so that the members can go out and start new groups.

Like the separation decision, a decision to cease operations should be made only after considerable discussion and mature discernment.

– CLIP IN –
"READY"
006

Community is risky. But the kinds of men we are—who we *truly* are—run *toward* danger, not away from it. We run toward danger when something of great value hangs in the balance. And, brother, something of great value *is* hanging in the balance: our well-being, the well-being of our friends and families, our companies, our communities.

When we face our fears, things happen. One becomes two. Two become three. And before we know it, we're a team. A mighty movement of men. A mighty movement of deep, durable men experiencing something one hundred times better than we can find anywhere else.

And then we realize that the biggest risk is not to take the risk of getting into community. The biggest risk is to "be conformed to this world" (Rom. 12:2). It's to trust this culture of darkness more than we trust Jesus.

Commit to making each of these bold moves.

006.1   What struck you about this chapter or in Curtis's story? Pull out a pen or pencil or your phone and describe whatever stood out to you personally.

006.2   Email or text a man—*someone God has put on your heart for this next season.* Do it today. Set up a call or a Zoom or a breakfast or a lunch or a time to grab coffee. Invite him into a conversation about community. And if after the meeting you discern that moving forward makes sense, ask him to start a group with you. Ask him to form a rescue team.

006.3   Schedule a follow-up meeting and have another conversation, this time a prayerful one, considering some or all of the following questions:

- What should our expectations be around commitment, size, open or closed?
- How should our group function, and what might be its focus?
- Who will lead, and how will decisions be made?
- How will conflicts be handled, and what rules might we want to adopt?

006.4   When the timing is right, schedule another meeting where you can tell each other your stories. Start at the beginning. Spend about an hour on each of you. Be as honest and vulnerable as possible. These are opportunities to provide context, but for confession too. "We must admit to our community … who we are at our worst," wrote Larry Crabb. "We must tell our stories to someone without consciously leaving out a chapter."[34] Doing all of this will set a good, solid foundation upon which your group can grow.

BEFORE YOU GO

In interviews I'm sometimes asked, "What's your best advice for men?" My response is always the same: "Get into community."

Find a few good men. Find one. And be honest. Get vulnerable. As best you can, talk about your past. Talk about your fears and struggles—the old ones and the ones you're facing right now. And confess your sins. Confess until it stings. And then take an interest in your brothers. Be curious: Who are they? What are *their* fears and struggles? But don't judge them. Love them. Sacrifice for them. Lay down your life for them, even if that just means sacrificing a few hours of your busy week to come together. And of course, if *laying down your life* requires more, do more.

Let the cavalry come, brother. I know it's hard. It was for me. (It's *still* hard.) But these times in which we live are evil, and we simply need a lot more of God in our lives—and this is the best way to get more. We need to experience his presence and glory on a more regular basis. We need to tap into more of his wisdom and help and love. We need to see miracles, and this is the best way.

I'll say it again: We're meant to *be* together, to *do life* together, to *care* for one another, to be *united* with God and our brothers and sisters in Jesus Christ.

And when we are united, then we are strong and healthy and free—even in the midst of the worst of circumstances. Lieutenant Cummings knew this in his heart. I do too. I too have experienced the fruit of living this way. One hundred times, remember? I pray you experience it as well.

Justin Camp
San Francisco Peninsula

ACKNOWLEDGMENTS

Thank you, again and always, to Jennifer, my wife, coconspirator, and dearest friend. Community, for me, always begins with you.

Special thanks to Wendi Lord, Michael Covington, and Kevin Kim. You believed in me and made this book series possible. Thank you also to the David C Cook team: Michael (again), Stephanie Bennett, Jeff Gerke, and Jack Campbell. You guys are pros. I'm honored to have such kind, talented partners.

Thank you to Nick Lee for another awesome cover and Dave Ewing, my friend and our creative director at Gather Ministries, for all those amazing map images.

Thank you to my mom, dad, and sister—for your soft hearts and strong faith.

Thank you to the men of the Oaks, the Deep, the Table, and the Cave. Thank you for being my brothers.

Thank you to Heather and C. J. Fitzgerald, our great friends and biggest champions. Without you, nothing we do at Gather would be possible.

And to my King, Jesus Christ, thank you most of all. Thank you for your impossible nearness.

NOTES

BEFORE YOU START

1. Carlos Romulo, *I Saw the Fall of the Philippines* (New York: Doubleday, 1942), 263.

2. Sidney Stewart, *Give Us This Day* (New York: W. W. Norton, 1956), 85.

3. "Heroic Chaplain of Bataan Dead," *New York Times*, October 6, 1945, 11.

4. Stewart, *Give Us This Day*, 164–65.

5. "Father William T. Cummings," Maryknoll Mission Archives, April 23, 2014, maryknollmissionarchives.org/deceased-fathers-bro/father-william-t-cummings-mm/.

CHAPTER 1: FAUX STONE AND LEATHER AND FREEDOM

1. Parker J. Palmer, "The Clearness Committee: A Communal Approach to Discernment in Retreats," Center for Courage and Renewal, accessed June 9, 2021, www.couragerenewal.org/clearnesscommittee/.

2. Parker J. Palmer, *Let Your Life Speak: Listening for the Voice of Vocation* (San Francisco: Jossey-Bass, 2000), 92.

3. Fyodor Dostoyevsky, *The Brothers Karamazov* (New York: Macmillan, 1922), 335.

CHAPTER 2: ROTORS AND CARABINERS AND RADIANCE

1. See www.rega.ch/en/about-us/rega-in-brief#facts-and-figures; www.air-glaciers.ch/carte-de-sauvetage; https://fr.wikipedia.org/wiki/Unit%C3%A9s_de_montagne_de_la_Gendarmerie_nationale; https://it.wikipedia.org/wiki/Corpo_nazionale_soccorso_alpino_e_speleologico.

2. "*The Horn*—Season 1," Red Bull, accessed June 10, 2021, www.redbull.com/us-en/videos/the-horn-season-1-trailer.

3. John Eldredge, *Get Your Life Back: Everyday Practices for a World Gone Mad* (Nashville, TN: Nelson Books, 2020), xiii.

4. Harry A. Ironside, *The Four Hundred Silent Years: From Malachi to Matthew* (Columbia, SC: Solid Christian Books, 2020), 83.

5. Ironside, *Four Hundred Silent Years*, 83.

6. A. W. Tozer, *The Attributes of God: Deeper into the Father's Heart*, vol. 2 (Chicago: Moody, 2015), 137.

7. *Strong's Exhaustive Concordance* and *HELPS Word-studies*, s.v. "hosanna," Bible Hub, accessed July 6, 2020, https://biblehub.com/greek/5614.htm.

8. NIV.

9. *HELPS Word-studies*, s.v. "sózó," Bible Hub, accessed July 6, 2020, https://biblehub.com/str/greek/4982.htm.

10. *Strong's Exhaustive Concordance* and *HELPS Word-studies*, s.v. "iaomai," Bible Hub, accessed July 6, 2020, https://biblehub.com/str/greek/2390.htm; *Strong's Exhaustive Concordance* and *HELPS Word-studies*, s.v. "therapeuó," Bible Hub, accessed July 6, 2020, https://biblehub.com/str/greek/2323.htm.

11. MSG.

12. N. T. Wright, *Jesus and the Victory of God: Christian Origins and the Question of God*, vol. 2 (Minneapolis, MN: Fortress, 1996), 401.

13. Sidney Stewart, *Give Us This Day* (New York: W. W. Norton, 1956), 165.

14. Parker J. Palmer, *A Place Called Community*, pamphlet (Wallingford, PA: Pendle Hill, 1977), 5.

15. MSG.

16. Dietrich Bonhoeffer, quoted in Charles E. Moore, comp. and ed., *Called to Community: The Life Jesus Wants for His People* (Walden, NY: Plough, 2016), 246.

17. MSG.

18. Larry Crabb, *Becoming a True Spiritual Community: A Profound Vision of What the Church Can Be* (Nashville, TN: Thomas Nelson, 1999), 177.

19. Crabb, *Becoming a True Spiritual Community*, 178.

CHAPTER 3: HOISTS AND FINS AND FRATERNITY

1. "Civilian Rescue," Igor I. Sikorsky Historical Archives, accessed June 12, 2021, www.sikorskyarchives.com/Civilian_Rescue.php.

2. "Civilian Rescue," www.sikorskyarchives.com/Civilian_Rescue.php.

3. "Civilian Rescue," www.sikorskyarchives.com/Civilian_Rescue.php.

4. "Joseph Pawlik: 29 November 1945," This Day in Aviation, November 29, 2020, www.thisdayinaviation.com/tag/joseph-pawlik/.

5. Mario Vittone, quoted in Martha J. LaGuardia-Kotite, *So Others May Live: Coast Guard's Rescue Swimmers: Saving Lives, Defying Death* (Guilford, CT: Lyons Press, 2006), 133.

6. WYC.

7. Gerald R. Hoover, *Brotherhood of the Fin: A Coast Guard Rescue Swimmer's Story* (Tucson, AZ: Wheatmark, 2007), 83.

8. Hoover, *Brotherhood of the Fin*, 83.

9. Patrick M. Morley, *The Man in the Mirror: Solving the 24 Problems Men Face* (Grand Rapids, MI: Zondervan, 2014), 163.

10. *The Works of George Swinnock* (London: T. Parkhurst, 1665), 319.

11. "Coast Guard Swimmers Test Boundaries of Courage," CBN, April 20, 2015, www1.cbn.com/coast-guard-swimmers-test-boundaries-courage.

12. "Cockpit Communication," *Coast Guard Compass*, blog, March 11, 2012, compass.coastguard.blog/2012/03/11/cockpit-communication/.

13. M. Scott Peck, *The Different Drum: Community Making and Peace* (New York: Touchstone, 1987), 70.

14. Fyodor Dostoyevsky, *The Brothers Karamazov* (New York: Macmillan, 1922), 322.

15. Dostoyevsky, *Brothers Karamazov*, 321–22.

16. "George Washington Papers, Series 3, Varick Transcripts, 1775–1785, Subseries 3B, Continental and State Military Personnel, 1775–1783, Letterbook 16: Dec. 1, 1782–June 11, 1785," Library of Congress, accessed June 12, 2021, www.loc.gov/item/mgw3b.016/.

17. "George Washington Papers," www.loc.gov/item/mgw3b.016/.

18. Thomas Paine, *Common Sense*, Internet Archive, accessed June 12, 2021, archive.org/details/commonsense00painrich/page/60/mode/2up.

19. Joshua Zeitz, "How World War II Almost Broke American Politics," *Politico Magazine*, June 6, 2019, www.politico.com/magazine/story/2019/06/06/how-world-war-ii-almost-broke-american-politics-227090.

20. Zeitz, "World War II," www.politico.com/magazine/story/2019/06/06/how-world-war-ii-almost-broke-american-politics-227090.

21. "Winston Churchill to President Harry S Truman, May 9, 1945," telegram, Library of Congress, accessed June 12, 2021, www.loc.gov/exhibits/churchill/wc-unity.html#232.

22. "FDR's D-Day Prayer," National Archives and Records Administration, June 5, 2019, fdr.blogs.archives.gov/2019/06/05/fdrs-d-day-prayer/, 3.

23. "World War II Poster Collection," Northwestern University, accessed June 12, 2021, dc.library.northwestern.edu/collections/faf4f60e-78e0-4fbf-96ce-4ca8b4df597a; David Vergun, "WWII Posters Aimed to Inspire, Encourage Service," US Department of Defense, October 16, 2019, www.defense.gov/Explore/Features/Story/Article/1990131/wwii-posters-aimed-to-inspire-encourage-service/.

24. "The Connection between Friendship and Fatherhood," Barna Group, June 10, 2020, www.barna.com/research/friendship-and-fatherhood/.

25. MSG.

26. Dallas Willard, *The Spirit of the Disciplines: Understanding How God Changes Lives* (New York: Harper, 1991), xii.

27. Morley, *Man in the Mirror*, 162.

28. Morley, *Man in the Mirror*, 164.

29. Morley, *Man in the Mirror*, 163.

30. Dietrich Bonhoeffer, *Life Together*, trans. John W. Doberstein (San Francisco: HarperOne, 1954), 20.

CHAPTER 4: DSVS AND ROVS AND TRUST

1. Rufus Jones, quoted in Charles E. Moore, comp. and ed., *Called to Community: The Life Jesus Wants for His People* (Walden, NY: Plough, 2016), 10.

2. Henri Nouwen, "From Solitude to Community to Ministry," *Leadership Journal*, spring 1995, www.christianitytoday.com/pastors/1995/spring/5l280.html.

3. Henri Nouwen, quoted in Charles E. Moore, comp. and ed., *Called to Community: The Life Jesus Wants for His People* (Walden, NY: Plough, 2016), 137.

4. Eberhard Arnold and Thomas Merton, *Why We Live in Community* (Walden, NY: Plough, 1995), 39.

5. C. S. Lewis, *The Four Loves* (San Francisco, HarperOne, 1960), 115.

6. Eugene Peterson, foreword, in Larry Crabb, *Becoming a True Spiritual Community: A Profound Vision of What the Church Can Be* (Nashville, TN: Thomas Nelson, 1999), viii.

7. Crabb, *Becoming a True Spiritual Community*, 165.

8. Eugene Peterson, quoted in Charles E. Moore, comp. and ed., *Called to Community: The Life Jesus Wants for His People* (Walden, NY: Plough, 2016), 280.

9. Dietrich Bonhoeffer, *Life Together*, trans. John W. Doberstein (San Francisco: HarperOne, 1954), 20.

10. Ian Traynor, "They Pray. They Hope. But They Fear That Their Sons Are Dead," *Guardian*, August 16, 2000, www.theguardian.com/world/2000/aug/17/kursk.russia3.

11. "Exercise Dynamic Monarch 2017—Soundbite 2," NATO Channel, Defense Visual Information Distribution Service, September 1, 2017, www.dvidshub.net/video/embed/558078.

12. Dietrich Bonhoeffer, *Life Together*, trans. John W. Doberstein (San Francisco: HarperOne, 1954), 29.

13. Dietrich Bonhoeffer, quoted in Charles E. Moore, comp. and ed., *Called to Community: The Life Jesus Wants for His People* (Walden, NY: Plough, 2016), 245.

14. Brené Brown, *Daring Greatly: How the Courage to Be Vulnerable Transforms the Way We Live, Parent, and Lead* (New York: Gotham Books, 2012), 69.

15. M. Scott Peck, *The Different Drum: Community Making and Peace* (New York: Touchstone, 1987), 67.

16. Peck, *Different Drum*, 68.

17. Lewis, *Four Loves*, 174.

18. Eberhard Arnold, quoted in Charles E. Moore, comp. and ed., *Called to Community: The Life Jesus Wants for His People* (Walden, NY: Plough, 2016), 108.

19. Parker J. Palmer, *A Place Called Community*, pamphlet (Wallingford, PA: Pendle Hill, 1977), 11.

20. David Dusek, *Rough Cut Men: A Man's Battle Guide to Building Real Relationships with Each Other, and with Jesus* (Issaquah, WA: Made for Success, 2015), 63.

CHAPTER 5: SAWS AND TORCHES AND DEVOTION

1. Brendan McDonough, *Granite Mountain: The Firsthand Account of a Tragic Wildfire, Its Lone Survivor, and the Firefighters Who Made the Ultimate Sacrifice* (New York: Hachette, 2016), 116.

2. John N. Maclean, *Fire on the Mountain: The True Story of the South Canyon Fire* (New York: Harper Perennial, 1999), 65.

3. Maclean, *Fire on the Mountain*, 64.

4. Maclean, *Fire on the Mountain*, 65.

5. "Hotshots Help Fight California Fires," *University Journal* (Cedar City, UT), November 1, 2007, 1, 6.

6. Emphasis added.

7. "Dallas Willard's Definitions," comp. Bill Gaultiere, Soul Shepherding, March 31, 2020, www.soulshepherding.org/dallas-willards-definitions/.

8. MSG.

9. Richard Rohr, *Near Occasions of Grace* (Maryknoll, NY: Orbis Books, 1993), 50.

10. Sidney Stewart, *Give Us This Day* (New York: W. W. Norton, 1956), 36.

11. Charles E. Moore, comp. and ed., *Called to Community: The Life Jesus Wants for His People* (Walden, NY: Plough, 2016), xxi.

12. McDonough, *Granite Mountain*, 267.

13. National IHC Steering Committee, *Hotshot Crew History in America* (2018), Wildfire Today, https://wildfiretoday.com/documents/Hotshot_Crew_History_2018.pdf, 116.

14. "Adam Hernandez," Smokey Generation, May 2014, thesmokeygeneration.com/view-stories-by-person/adam-hernandez/.

15. "Dan Pickard," Smokey Generation, May 2014, thesmokeygeneration.com/view-stories-by-person/dan-pickard/.

16. Murray Bodo, *The Way of St. Francis: The Challenge of Franciscan Spirituality for Everyone* (Cincinnati, OH: St. Anthony Messenger Press, 1995), 118.

17. Dan Allender, quoted in Morgan Snyder, *Becoming a King: The Path to Restoring the Heart of a Man* (Nashville, TN: W Publishing, 2020), 167.

18. Eberhard Arnold and Thomas Merton, *Why We Live in Community* (Walden, NY: Plough, 1995), 39.

19. Moore, *Called to Community*, 89.

20. Moore, *Called to Community*, 89.

21. "Flathead Hotshots Travel to Canada to Fight Wildfires," YouTube, uploaded by KPAX-TV, June 4, 2019, https://youtu.be/t4g8RJrihLU.

22. McDonough, *Granite Mountain*, 87.

23. McDonough, *Granite Mountain*, 87.

24. Rudyard Kipling, *The Second Jungle Book* (New York: Century, 1895), 29, quoted in National IHC Steering Committee, *Hotshot Crew History in America* (2018), Wildfire Today, https://wildfiretoday.com/documents/Hotshot_Crew_History_2018.pdf, 55.

25. Patrick M. Morley, *The Man in the Mirror: Solving the 24 Problems Men Face* (Grand Rapids, MI: Zondervan, 2014), 171.

26. *Strong's Greek Concordance*, s.v. "koinónia," Bible Hub, accessed June 13, 2021, biblehub.com/greek/2842.htm.

27. C. S. Lewis, *The Grand Miracle* (New York: Ballantine Books, 1970), 24.

28. C. S. Lewis, *The Joyful Christian* (New York: Simon & Schuster, 1977), 197–98.

29. Morley, *Man in the Mirror*, 125.

30. MSG.

31. Eberhard Arnold and Thomas Merton, *Why We Live in Community* (Walden, NY: Plough, 1995), 42.

CHAPTER 6: BARS AND BIBLES AND CONFIDENCE

1. *Monthly Report of Population as of Midnight April 30, 2020*, California Department of Corrections and Rehabilitation, Division of Internal Oversight and Research (2020).

2. Paige St. John, "A Rare Peek at San Quentin's Death Row, and Conversations with Inmates Awaiting Their Fates as Political Battles Swirl," *Los Angeles Times*, December 29, 2015.

3. Mark Gladstone, "San Quentin 'Decrepit,'" *San Jose Mercury News*, April 14, 2005.

4. *Monthly Report of Population as of Midnight April 30, 2020*, California Department of Corrections and Rehabilitation, Division of Internal Oversight and Research (2020).

5. "United States Military Chaplains," Wikipedia, April 22, 2021, https://en.wikipedia.org/wiki/United_States_military_chaplains#cite_note-1.

6. "Navy Chaplain," America's Navy, accessed June 14, 2021, www.navy.com/careers/navy-chaplain.

7. "United States Military Chaplains," https://en.wikipedia.org/wiki/United_States_military_chaplains#cite_note-1.

8. *Religion in Prisons: A 50-State Survey of Prison Chaplains*, Pew Research Center, March 22, 2012, www.pewresearch.org/wp-content/uploads/sites/7/2012/03/Religion-in-Prisons.pdf, 7.

9. Kenneth Lamott, *Chronicles of San Quentin: The Biography of a Prison*, ebook (San Francisco: Muriwai Books, 2018).

10. Lamott, *Chronicles of San Quentin*, ebook.

11. Benjamin Justice, "'A College of Morals': Educational Reform at San Quentin Prison, 1880–1920," *History of Education Quarterly*, vol. 40, no. 3 (2000), 282.

12. *Religion in Prisons: A 50-State Survey of Prison Chaplains*, Pew Research Center, March 22, 2012, www.pewresearch.org/wp-content/uploads/sites/7/2012/03/Religion-in-Prisons.pdf.

13. Earl Smith, *Death Row Chaplain: Unbelievable True Stories from America's Most Notorious Prison*, ebook (New York: Howard Books, 2015).

14. "Chaplaincy at the BOP," video, Federal Bureau of Prisons, accessed June 30, 2021, www.bop.gov/jobs/positions/index.jsp?p=Chaplain.

15. Smith, *Death Row Chaplain*, ebook.

16. A. W. Tozer, *Church: Living Faithfully as the People of God* (Chicago: Moody, 2019), 92.

17. First Generation Quakers at Balby, quoted in Eberhard Arnold and Thomas Merton, *Why We Live in Community* (Walden, NY: Plough, 1995), vii.

18. Basil Pennington, foreword, in Arnold and Merton, *Why We Live in Community*, xiii.

19. Edith Schaeffer, quoted in Charles E. Moore, comp. and ed., *Called to Community: The Life Jesus Wants for His People* (Walden, NY: Plough, 2016), 306.

20. M. Scott Peck, *The Different Drum: Community Making and Peace* (New York: Touchstone, 1987), 64.

21. Peck, *Different Drum*, 63.

22. Gerhard Lohfink, *Jesus and Community: The Social Dimension of Christian Faith*, trans. John P. Galvin (Philadelphia: Fortress Press, 1984), 122.

23. Dietrich Bonhoeffer, *Life Together*, trans. John W. Doberstein (San Francisco: HarperOne, 1954), 114.

24. Bonhoeffer, *Life Together*, 111.

25. Bonhoeffer, *Life Together*, 113.

26. Bonhoeffer, *Life Together*, 111.

27. Larry Crabb, *Becoming a True Spiritual Community: A Profound Vision of What the Church Can Be* (Nashville, TN: Thomas Nelson, 1999), 173–74.

28. MSG.

29. MSG.

30. A. W. Tozer, *Church: Living Faithfully as the People of God* (Chicago: Moody, 2019), 119.

31. Bonhoeffer, *Life Together*, 44.

32. Bonhoeffer, *Life Together*, 108.

33. Peck, *Different Drum*, 160.

34. Crabb, *Becoming a True Spiritual Community*, 31.

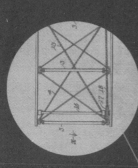
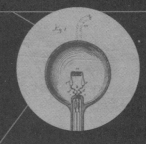
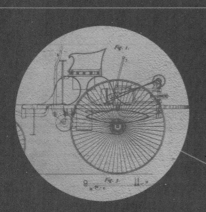